ECONOMICS INVESTIGATED

Data and Issues in A Level Economics

Robert Paisley and John Quillfeldt

COLLINS
EDUCATIONAL

© Robert Paisley and John Quillfeldt 1989

ISBN 0 00 327392 X

Published 1989 by Collins Educational, 8 Grafton Street, London W1X 3LA.

Reprinted 1990

Design, figures and cover by John Fitzmaurice

Typeset by Burns & Smith, Derby, and
printed and bound by Butler and Tanner., Frome, Somerset

Contents

Introduction

Acknowledgements

Introduction

AIMS

The book is designed to help students become proficient in the understanding, interpretation and analysis of economic data. It will also encourage students to understand and analyse a range of contemporary issues using the knowledge and skills acquired on GCE A level economics courses. The presentation and approach of the book is designed to be readily accessible to students who have experienced a GCSE approach to teaching and learning.

USING THE BOOK

The book is designed to complement, and to be used in conjunction with, a core GCE A level textbook such as *Economics Explained*. It is divided up into thirty-seven, self-contained, double-page units. However, the book is not intended to be a systematic teaching package that must be worked through from beginning to end. Readers may attempt units at whatever time seems appropriate during their A level course. Teachers and students can, of course, be selective not only in the order in which they undertake units, but also in the way they approach the work assignments within each unit.

THE DATA

The items of data have been chosen with several criteria in mind. They have been selected from both primary and secondary sources to reflect the type of economic information that readers are likely to meet both in examinations and in their future lives as consumers and producers. In addition, they reflect many different methods in the presentation of data to allow students to develop a variety of data analysis skills. Finally, they have been chosen to present lively and interesting perspectives on the economic issues under consideration.

THE WORK ASSIGNMENTS

- The 'Data Analysis Skills' sections are designed to help readers understand and interpret data. Some of the skills are covered in several units because they are a source of repeated errors among many students.
- Questions in the 'Applying Economic Principles' sections help students to explore the relationship between economic theory and real world issues. Each question is stepped in difficulty where possible, and the later questions in each section may be more demanding than the earlier questions.
- Suggestions in the 'For Further Investigation' sections may be used in two main ways: as the basis for project or assignment work, and as a stimulating alternative to going over examination questions. Brief reference is made in most cases to appropriate primary and secondary sources, but it should be the student's task to find out where to obtain relevant information.
- Each unit has an 'Essay' section containing two essay questions. The first is designed to encourage students to select from the data in the unit to answer the question. The second title is taken, wherever possible, from a recent A level examination paper.

1 The housing market

Going through the roof

Figure 1.1
House prices — First quarter 1988

Northern Ireland
1 (30)
Scotland
5 (36)
North West
22
11
11 (35)
18
34
Wales (42)
West Midlands
55
South West
28
7
North (31)
9
Yorkshire & Humberside (31)
40 East Midlands
39
26
23 (80)
59 East Anglia
Greater London
South East (74)

0 % increase on a year ago

Average price
(00) £'000

Source: Halifax Building Society

Figure 1.2
Changes in house and retail prices compared

Retail prices ••••••
House prices ▬▬▬▬

% rise each year
40
38
30
22
14
6
2
0

1957 1961 1965 1969 1973 1977 1981 86 87 88

Source: Halifax Building Society, Guardian 21 July 1987

Figure 1.3

Dinky dwellings at dotty prices

SEVERAL building societies are now betting that house prices in London will continue to outstrip buyers' incomes and house prices in the rest of the country for the next few years:

● Demographic changes favour house prices in the South East. For example, the government has forecast that between now and the year 2001, the number of households will rise by a third in Buckinghamshire, while on Merseyside the number will fall slightly. With the supply of houses in the South East limited by the green belt, this will keep upward pressure on prices.

● The traditional link between incomes and house prices may have changed in recent years because house buyers are now able to borrow a much bigger multiple of their incomes. A quarter of all new purchasers in London now take on loans of more than four times their annual incomes; in the 1970s, a multiple of more than two and a half was rare.

● The Halifax building society's survey shows that two-thirds of all the mortgages of first-time buyers in London are supported by more than one income; in Yorkshire and Humberside, only

a third. The "dinky" (double-income-no-kids-yet) phenomenon, where a two-salary couple can afford to pay twice as much as a single person for the same accommodation, has helped to keep London's first-time-buyers market buoyant.

In addition, an increasing number of houses and flats are being bought jointly by young single people, who individually could barely afford a broom cupboard. Building societies treat such joint applications much more favourably than they did a decade ago.

Source: *The Economist* 18 July 1987

Figure 1.4

Builders set sights on guidelines for growth

THE Government should state clearly how many new houses will be needed over the next five years, and where they should go. It should also set up land agencies in London and other conurbations to assemble sites for builders, and double its spending on urban aid, according to a report by the industry.

The recommendations are from a commission set up by the House-Builders Federation to assess the scope for inner city building and meet the charge of builders preferring the "easy option" of building on greenfield sites. Its study of 12 areas has taken 14 months.

The team, headed by Mr Wyndham Thomas, the former general manager of Peterborough New Town, concludes that there is much less inner city land suitable for private building than is commonly held; that low-cost housing is needed for local people; and that building in the inner cities will not significantly divert pressure for new houses in the countryside.

The report, which forecasts continued migration from London to the shire counties, will be used by house-builders to back their demands for more housing land in the rural South East.

It also projects the image of an industry working largely in the dark in the inner cities and the country. There is a serious lack of reliable information on the amount, availability and suitability of vacant land, and on the demand for new houses. Scarcer still is information on the different housing markets and how they interact.

House-builders should do more research, particularly into the needs of ethnic minorities. Extended families, religious and other customs often make existing house types unsuitable for these groups.

The report has a long list of suggestions for helping to increase the inner city housebuilding from the current level of below 10 per cent — releasing and assembling land, raising public investment to stimulate the private sector, and better forecasting of demand.

Private house-building should be seen as a necessary part of urban regeneration for its own sake, not as a means of saving land outside the city, it says.

Research for the commission by Dr

Margaret Anderson, of London University's Wye College in Kent, shows that rural land is being taken for building of all kinds at about 12,350 acres a year, compared with more than 70,000 acres in the 1970s.

On optimistic assumptions about economic growth, she forecasts an increase to about 22,000 acres by 1990, falling back through the decade to about 12,000 acres.

In the South East the proportion of land in urban use rose from 11.9 per cent in 1954 to 15.7 per cent in 1981 and could on present trends reach about 17 per cent by the year 2,000, she says.

Lifting housing growth in London, through building and conversion, from the current 15,000 a year to 20,000 a year would be a major and welcome achievement, the report says.

But there would not be a commensurate reduction of demand outside. Relatively few of the households wanting to buy in towns and villages outside London are likely to turn to inner London. Few could afford to do so at present prices, and many will in any case be working outside London.

Source: John Ardill, *Guardian* 17 July 1987

Figure 1.1
Regional variations can mask local variations. For the purpose of economic analysis, the government divides up the country into eleven main planning regions. Other organizations, such as building societies, may use the same regions for statistical analysis. It must be remembered that the regions are not uniform, and that there may be significant variations within them. For example, unemployment may vary as much within a region as between regions.

1. What was the average house price in the first quarter of 1988 in (a) the South East, and (b) Greater London?

2. Greater London counts as part of the South East: was the average house price in the South East outside Greater London higher or lower than your answer to **1** (a)? Explain your answer.

Figure 1.2
Changes over long periods of time should be analysed by dividing them into periods which have common features. When analysing statistics it is important to try and avoid just repeating the statistics in prose form. Patterns and trends within statistics should be identified, and figures should be used only to illustrate them. Look for time periods with common features, even if a large number of years are involved, and treat them as a single period.

3. Why should 1958 to 1970 be treated as a single period for the purpose of describing trends in the statistics?

4. Describe the trends in house prices after 1970.

Figure 1.3
Newspaper and magazine articles may contain many economic points without using technical economic terms. Journalists often discuss economic events without using the economic terms that a student would learn on an economics course. Using the 'jargon' could put off the general reader. It is important, however, to be able to identify the economic points in articles intended for general readership. Economists might analyse this passage with reference to the conditions of demand. Other economic concepts are less obviously present but may be hinted at — for example, government intervention in the housing market exemplified by the 'green belt'.

5. What do economists call the factors other than price which affect the demand for a good? List two such factors that appear in this article.

6. Identify one other economic concept suggested by the passage.

Figure 1.4
The source of research may affect conclusions. Not all research is necessarily neutral and unbiased. Pressure groups may commission research and set terms of reference in a way that will support their interests. On other occasions they may latch on to independent reports whose conclusions lend support to their views. There is nothing wrong with pressure groups using research to back their case, but it is important to recognize where this is occurring.

7. Which group commissioned the research, and what did they hope it would achieve?

APPLYING ECONOMIC PRINCIPLES

1. Refer to Figure 1.1. (a) In which region of the country did the demand for housing appear to be highest relative to the supply in 1988? Explain your answer. (b) (i) What is meant by 'declining traditional staple industries'? (ii) Give two examples of such industries, and regions in which they were particularly important. (iii) Explain the link between these industries and the house prices shown.

2. With reference to Figures 1.3 and 1.4: (a) Referring to specific conditions of demand, describe how demand conditions can help to explain house price differentials throughout the country. (b) Which policies of (i) the government, and (ii) the building societies have helped to boost demand for houses? Give reasons for your answer.

3. Refer to Figure 1.2. (a) House price changes are thought to be a good indicator of economic activity in general. In which three periods were economic conditions relatively buoyant? Explain your answer. (b) What is meant by income elasticity of demand? (c) Is income elasticity of demand positive or negative (i) for normal goods, (ii) for housing? Ex-plain your answers. (d) State the difference between 'real' and 'money' (or 'nominal') house prices. (e) In which years were house prices (i) rising in money terms, and (ii) falling in real terms? Explain your answer.

4. Refer to Figures 1.3 and 1.4. (a) What supply factors were affecting the housing market in 1988? (b) Which of the factors affect housing supply (i) in the short term, and (ii) in the long term? (c) Draw a supply and demand diagram to show why house prices were rising so rapidly in the South East in 1988. (d) (i) Why did the House-Builders Federation feel that more housebuilding in the countryside was required? (ii) What measures could the government take to release more rural land? (e) What would be the possible (i) external costs, (ii) external benefits of more rural land being released for housing?

5 (a) What is meant by 'immobility in the labour market'? (b) How is labour immobility related to rigidities in the housing market? (c) What would be the possible effects on the labour market if the government ended all controls on building in the countryside?

FOR FURTHER INVESTIGATION
Free newspapers carry advertisements for property. Try to obtain a number of these newspapers covering as wide a geographical area as possible. Choose a particular kind of property and illustrate variations in its price between different areas using a bar chart, or some other method of statistical presentation. Using supply and demand analysis, write a report explaining the factors that could account for the variations in price that you have discovered.

ESSAYS
Refer to the data wherever possible, especially in the first essay.
1. 'House prices in the South East are far too high for people to afford.' Discuss.
2. How do (a) rent controls, and (b) tax relief on mortgages affect the market for housing? [London 1/87]

Metal fatigue

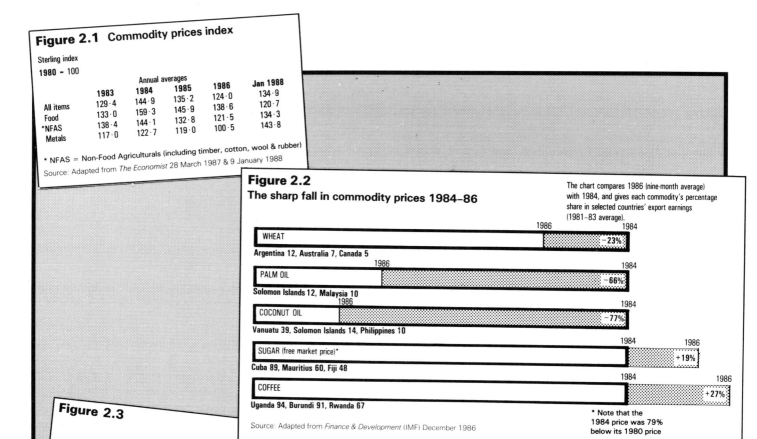

Figure 2.1 Commodity prices index

Sterling index
1980 = 100

		Annual averages		1986	Jan 1988
	1983	**1984**	**1985**	**1986**	**Jan 1988**
All items	129·4	144·9	135·2	124·0	134·9
Food	133·0	159·3	145·9	138·6	120·7
*NFAS	138·4	144·1	132·8	121·5	134·3
Metals	117·0	122·7	119·0	100·5	143·8

* NFAS = Non-Food Agriculturals (including timber, cotton, wool & rubber)

Source: Adapted from *The Economist* 28 March 1987 & 9 January 1988

Figure 2.2
The sharp fall in commodity prices 1984–86

The chart compares 1986 (nine-month average) with 1984, and gives each commodity's percentage share in selected countries' export earnings (1981–83 average).

WHEAT — 1986 / 1984 **−23%**
Argentina 12, Australia 7, Canada 5

PALM OIL — 1986 / 1984 **−66%**
Solomon Islands 12, Malaysia 10

COCONUT OIL — 1986 / 1984 **−77%**
Vanuatu 39, Solomon Islands 14, Philippines 10

SUGAR (free market price)* — 1984 / 1986 **+19%**
Cuba 89, Mauritius 60, Fiji 48

COFFEE — 1984 / 1986 **+27%**
Uganda 94, Burundi 91, Rwanda 67

* Note that the 1984 price was 79% below its 1980 price

Source: Adapted from *Finance & Development* (IMF) December 1986

Figure 2.3

Raw deal for raw materials

COMMODITY prices, like most other prices, are fixed by a mixture of supply, demand and government intervention.

Supply has expanded partly because of technological change, and partly because the expectation of higher prices in the 1970s led to increased investment and overcapacity. Technological change has also affected demand: cheap substitutes are now available for many primary commodities, especially metals. Meanwhile, government intervention—most notoriously in the food markets of America, Europe and Japan—has raised prices in industrial countries' markets. This has led to oversupply by industrial countries' producers, and in turn has reduced the free-market prices paid to farmers in developing countries who produce for export.

Because of its effect on both demand and supply, technological change may be the biggest single factor behind falling prices. High-yielding, disease-resistant varieties of plants—plus better fertilisers and pesticides—have turned India into a grain exporter. They are bringing China close to self-sufficiency. Technology has made the desert bloom in Saudi Arabia, so the country now produces roughly twice as much wheat as it needs.

In the industrial countries, technology is enabling farmers to crowd more crops into any patch of land than ever before. Governments sometimes attempt to reduce farm production by freezing or cutting support prices, only to find that their attempts are foiled by chemicals that drive crop yields up again. Demand for food has risen as fast as the scaremongers said it would, but technology has helped farmers to more than make up the difference.

The makers of everything from cars to coffee-pots are shunning metals in favour of new composite materials. The world's telecommunications companies are using fibre-optics to make cables where once they used copper wire. A 100-lb length of fibre cable can transmit as much information as a tonne of copper wire. More important, the amount of metal in each unit of manufacturing output is falling fast. Between 1979 and 1985, when manufacturing output grew by an average of 2.1% a year, world consumption of aluminium was static. During that period copper usage fell.

Source: *The Economist* 18 April 1987

Figure 2.1
Index numbers provide an easy method of recognizing percentage changes in values from a base date. Index numbers are a quick and easy way of seeing how a price has changed in percentage rather than absolute terms. An index number of (say) 150 for the Retail Prices Index indicates that the price of a typical basket of goods bought by a typical family has risen by 50 per cent since the base date. Care must be taken when comparing two index numbers if one of the index numbers is not 100: if an index number rises from 110 to 120, this is *not* a 10 per cent rise.

1. What was the percentage rise in food commodity prices between 1980 and 1986?

2. What was the percentage fall in metal commodity prices between 1985 and 1986?

Figure 2.2
Percentages increases and decreases can appear misleadingly dramatic if they start from a low base. The 'success' or 'failure' of things is often measured in percentage terms. This can be misleading. For example, if a political party with only two seats in the House of Commons gains two more seats in an election, the number of seats it holds would remain very small. It could claim, however, 'a dramatic 100 per cent increase' in its number of seats.

3. Which commodity had the highest percentage (a) rise in price, (b) fall in price from 1984 to 1986?

4. Explain why the performance of sugar may have been far less impressive than wheat as far as commodity traders were concerned between 1980 and 1986.

Figure 2.3
Newspaper and magazine articles may fail to distinguish between extensions and contractions in demand and supply, and shifts in demand and supply. Economists make a distinction between changes in demand and supply caused by changes in the price of a good, and changes caused by conditions *other* than a change in the price of a good. The way they show these changes on diagrams will be different in each case. However, these distinctions are not usually found outside economic textbooks.

5. The passage states that technological change has affected demand and supply. Explain one way in which technology can cause a rise in demand for a commodity, and one way in which it can cause an extension in demand for a commodity. Illustrate your answer with diagrams.

APPLYING ECONOMIC PRINCIPLES

1. With reference to Figure 2.1: (a) Describe the trends shown in commodity prices between 1980 and 1988. (b) Explain the difference between 'nominal' and 'real' price rises. (c) Did metal prices rise in (i) nominal, (ii) real terms between 1980 and 1986? Explain your answer. (d) Refer to Figure 1.3, and name one factor which would explain the very small rise in nominal metal prices between 1980 and 1986.

2. Commodities often have price inelastic supply curves. (a) (i) Explain why many commodities will have price inelastic supply curves. (ii) Illustrate in diagram form why changes in demand will have a greater effect on the price of goods with inelastic supply than on those with more elastic supply. (b) With reference to Figure 2.1: (i) Describe what happened to the price of metals between 1986 and 1988; (ii) Was this change more likely to have been caused by demand or supply changes? Give reasons for your answer.

3. Commodities often have price inelastic demand curves. (a) Explain why many food products will have price inelastic demand curves. (b) With reference to Figure 2.2: (i) Describe what happened to the price of sugar between 1980 and 1986.

(ii) Illustrate by diagram how unplanned fluctuations in sugar supply could lead to very large changes in the price of sugar.

4. Many commodities, like sugar, have their main markets in high income countries. As these countries become richer they may reduce their demand for sugar. (a) What is meant by 'income elasticity of demand'? (b) If the above statement about sugar is correct, has sugar a positive or negative income elasticity of demand? Explain your answer. (c) Would an exporting country prefer a positive or negative income elasticity of demand for its products? Give reasons for your answer.

5. With reference to Figure 2.2: (a) Name three countries that earn over 50 per cent of their export earnings from a single primary export; name the products concerned. (b) Explain why these countries have very unreliable sources of export earnings.

6. Using information in Figure 1.3, explain some of the ways in which technology can affect the demand and the supply of commodities.

FOR FURTHER INVESTIGATION
Gold prices are quoted in many newspapers. Keep a record of the price of gold over several months. In addition, keep a record of the price of one of the commodities shown in Figure 2.1, preferably a metal such as copper. Write a report comparing the price movements of gold with the other commodity. Explain what factors influence the price of gold, and why it is different from other commodities.

ESSAYS
Refer to the data wherever possible, especially in the first essay.
1. 'Developing countries will always be economically vulnerable until they reduce their dependence on commodity exports.' Discuss.
2. Why do the prices of some commodities fluctuate more than those of others? [London 6/87]

3 Centrally planned economies

yielding to the market

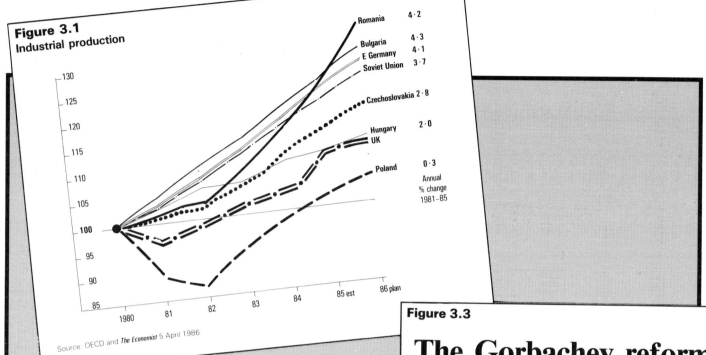

Figure 3.1
Industrial production

Romania 4·2
Bulgaria 4·3
E Germany 4·1
Soviet Union 3·7
Czechoslovakia 2·8
Hungary 2·0
UK
Poland 0·3

Annual % change 1981–85

Source: OECD and *The Economist* 5 April 1986

Figure 3.2
Soviet Union's Trade with the West

by volume 1981 = 100

Soviet exports

Soviet imports

by value
% change on a year ago

Soviet exports
Soviet imports

Source: United Nations and *The Economist* 6 December 1986

Figure 3.3

The Gorbachev reform

CAN the Soviet Union successfully reform itself to improve the economic efficiency of the system, and if it does so, will such a reform involve greater use of prices and markets? At present, the indications are not very clear, because most of what Gorbachev has actually done (as opposed to talked about in speeches or through the press) can be categorised as 'improving the centralised model'. By this I mean such measures as the campaign to eliminate corruption throughout the economy, and the campaigns to strengthen work discipline in factories and financial discipline on the part of enterprises. These can all be seen as attempts to strengthen central control over the economy.

On the other hand, Gorbachev has stressed the need for greater flexibility in the economy and more rapid innovation, and he has allowed quite radical reform proposals to be published in normally conservative journals. Thus he is well aware of the deep-seated problem facing the Soviet economy and must therefore know that the measures recently announced do no more than scratch the surface. For instance, the proposal to relax restrictions on private sector economic activity is significant and welcome, but will do little by itself to boost the economy's productivity, not least because the restrictions that remain are still very strong. (The reform is far more cautious than Hungary's 1980 measures, or reforms recently implemented in China.)

A more interesting and important reform, currently under discussion in the Soviet Union, is the introduction of trade in means of production. This means that the planners would abandon the current practice of administrative allocation of inputs to firms and simply allow firms to make their own supply arrangements through a system of markets. This measure was part of Hungary's 1968 reforms and on the whole it has worked well, freeing the planners to concentrate more on investment and other longer term issues. However, in the Soviet Union this sort of reform is still widely regarded as dangerously radical and it is not clear whether Gorbachev has yet established sufficient political authority to carry it through comprehensively. In any case, this would only be the first of a series of much needed reforms, at least some of which would strengthen the role of markets in Soviet economic management.

Source: *The Economic Review* November 1987

Figure 3.1
There are different ways of measuring economic 'success'. A country could assess economic 'success' in many ways; for example, by measuring the increase in industrial production (mineral extraction and secondary industry output), or total national production of all goods and services (the 'national income'), or by more specific measures like the number of cars, telephones, doctors etc per head of the population. Care must be taken in interpreting percentage increases in indicators of economic welfare: a country that starts from a very low base could record spectacular increases in performance in percentage terms, following a comparatively moderate absolute improvement in the indicator. For example, a country with only 100 telephones would increase its telephones by 100 per cent if it installed just 100 more.

1. Explain how well the line graphs would represent the success of a country that had enjoyed a larger than average growth in its service sector over the years shown.

2. Can it be inferred that Romania had a larger industrial output in 1986 than the UK? Explain your answer.

Figure 3.2
A distinction must be made between volume and value. Volume refers to the quantity of something, e.g. by weight or by units. Value is the money value of a given quantity. A firm might find, for example, that it is selling 10 per cent more cars each year, but if the price of cars had fallen by over 10 per cent, the value of the cars it sells would actually have fallen.

3. What happened to (a) the volume of Soviet exports, and (b) the value of Soviet exports in 1983?

4. Explain how the volume of Soviet imports could have risen in 1984 while the value fell.

Figure 3.3
Implicit assumptions may be made in articles. Writers sometimes believe that something is desirable or undesirable, and this influences the way that they write. They may not always state clearly what they are assuming to be desirable or undesirable. The writer in this passage assumes, for example, that the possibly greater volume of goods and services produced by the increased use of the market mechanism in a centrally planned economy is 'desirable'. Some people, particularly in a socialist society, would question that higher material living standards, as reflected by more consumer goods, are desirable.

5. What evidence can you find in the passage to suggest that this writer believes the market mechanism to be preferable to central control of the economy?

APPLYING ECONOMIC PRINCIPLES

1. Look at Figure 3.1. Do the data suggest that economic reform in the eastern European centrally planned economies is unnecessary? Explain your answer.

2. (a) In Figure 3.3, what is meant by the phrase: 'the introduction of trade in means of production'?
(b) Suggest three products that could be covered by this measure.
(c) Draw a supply and demand diagram for one of the products suggested in (b). (i) Indicate how a shortage could occur if the price is set by the government. (ii) Indicate and describe the economic effect of removing the restriction on the market.

3. What economic costs and benefits (both private and external) can result from the changes indicated in Figure 3.3?

4. (a) What are the implications of the changes shown in Figure 3.2 between 1985 and 1986 for (i) the Soviet Union, and (ii) the West? (b) How might the economic reforms in Figure 1.3 affect the trading positions of centrally planned economies with the West?

5. Economies like Soviet Union often have large black markets: (a) What is a 'black market'? (b) Why can black markets sometimes exist in centrally planned economies? (c) Do consumers benefit from the existence of black markets? Explain your answer. (d) How and why might the changes indicated in Figure 1.3 reduce the use of the black market in the Soviet Union?

FOR FURTHER INVESTIGATION
Newspapers, radio and television frequently carry reports of economic developments in the Soviet Union. Keep a record of these developments, and note particularly the problems of implementing change in the Soviet Union. Your record could be kept in the form of a scrapbook of cuttings, and notes you have made from radio and television reports. When you have collected a reasonable amount of information write a summary of your findings and analyse the extent to which the Soviet economy is being changed towards new methods of allocating resources.

ESSAYS
Refer to the data wherever possible, especially in the first essay.
1. (a) Describe some of the proposals made by Mr Gorbachev for changes in the operation of the Soviet economy, and explain why the changes have been proposed. (b) Do recent improvements in eastern bloc industrial production suggest that the proposals are unjustified?
2. How are resources allocated in (a) a free market and (b) a planned economy? Examine the relative merits, in terms of economic efficiency, of each method of resource allocation. [London 6/87]

4 Exchange rates

A fair exchange

Figure 4.1
Sterling exchange rates (end of December)

	1983	1984	1985	1986	1987	1988 (APR)
Sterling effective (1975 = 100)	83	73	78	69	76	78
ECU	1·75	1·64	1·63	1·38	1·44	1·51
SDR	1·38	1·18	1·32	1·21	1·32	1·35
$	1·45	1·16	1·45	1·48	1·83	1·88
Deutschmarks	3·95	3·64	3·54	2·85	2·98	3·14
Yen	337	290	299	235	230	236

Source: Various

Figure 4.2

Central banks drive European interest rates down to help $

WEST GERMANY and Britain led a concerted round of interest rate cuts by seven European nations yesterday in an attempt to halt the dollar's slide on foreign exchange markets and to restore confidence on world stock markets.

In London, the leading banks lowered their base rates by 0.5 percentage points to 8.5 per cent following a strong signal from the Bank of England. The reduction, the third since the stock market crash on October 19, took borrowing costs down to their lowest level since March 1984.

The West German Bundesbank also cut its key discount rate by 0.5 percentage points. The new rate of 2.5 per cent marks the lowest level seen since the beginning of the country's central banking history in 1876.

The move was described by Mr Gerhard Stoltenberg, West Germany's Finance Minister, as an im-

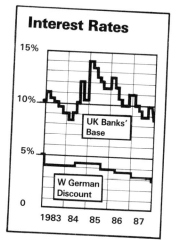

Interest Rates

portant contribution to the stabilisation of equity and foreign exchange markets. It was also a signal of the West German Government's commitment to international co-operation.

Central banks in France, Switzerland, Belgium, the Netherlands, and Austria followed the West German lead, reducing their official interest rates by between 0.25 and 0.5 points.

The Bank of England's move came slightly earlier than the West German action, but was taken with advance knowledge of the Bundesbank's intentions.

Mr Nigel Lawson, the Chancellor, emphasised the concerted nature of the interest rate cuts, and their contribution to wider international co-operation. Other European monetary officials were more cautious, however, suggesting that once the Bundesbank had decided to lower its discount rate, a more general downward shift was inevitable.

The Chancellor added that he

still hoped for an early meeting of finance ministers of the Group of Seven leading industrial nations. The key element in such a meeting, however, had to be a commitment — above all by the US — to take whatever action was needed to stabilise the dollar.

Yesterday Mr James Baker, the US Treasury Secretary, said the European action represented "an important contribution to our international economic policy co-ordination efforts."

European officials, however, remain uncertain whether the move — along with the budgetary measures announced by West Germany earlier this week — will be enough to persuade the US to give a firm pledge to support the dollar. In particular, European governments are seeking a commitment from Washington that it will, if necessary, raise interest rates.

Source: *Financial Times* 4 December 1987

Figure 4.3

G7 reaffirms desire for stable exchange rates

THE GROUP OF SEVEN leading industrial nations said yesterday that it hoped to avoid any further significant shifts in the dollar's value, but left financial markets guessing as to the extent that it would co-operate to prop up the US currency.

In a lengthy joint statement, the group re-emphasised its "common interest in more stable exchange rates".

It pledged close co-operation in implementing policies to strengthen the economic fundamentals that would underpin currency stability.

However, the seven — the US, Japan, West Germany, France, Britain, Italy and Canada — backed away from any specific commitment to joint action in support of the dollar. They dropped a key phrase in their February Louvre accord which had asserted that the dollar's fall since 1985 had brought

exchange rates into line with underlying economic conditions.

Senior officials involved in drafting the statement said that the new wording marked a compromise between the US and its partners.

While the European nations and Japan had sought a firm pledge on dollar stability, Washington insisted it would not give an open-ended commitment to defend its currency.

That difference, reflecting US concern that by raising interest rates to support the dollar it could push its economy towards recession, also explained the group's decision not to hold a formal meeting. Several ministers repeated yesterday that no such gathering was planned.

The bulk of the statement, released following President Ronald Reagan's decision to sign a $76bn package of

measures to reduce the US budget deficit, focuses on the group's declared intention to eliminate large international payments imbalances.

It gives a relatively optimistic assessment of progress so far towards cutting the huge US trade deficit and the surpluses of Japan and West Germany.

"The policies which have been implemented this year are gradually showing their intended effects," the statement says. "In particular, the balance between domestic demand and output in the United States and in Japan and the Federal Republic of Germany has shifted in a direction which promotes external adjustment."

The US deficit-cutting package, recent expansionary measures taken in West Germany and the Europe-wide cut in interest rates are singled out as a further step in the right direction. At

the same time Japan has pledged itself to maintain the recent strong growth rate in its economy.

Neither the US nor its partners, however, outline any new policy measures to be implemented over the next few months.

The officials acknowledged yesterday that there was still no consensus among the seven on an appropriate level for the dollar's value. They stressed, however, that there was an agreed ment, to which the US Treasury acceded, that a precipitate fall would be damaging.

They added that there was an implicit understanding that central banks would intervene if necessary to prevent a sharp decline in the dollar's value but that the banks would not necessarily be defending a specific target range

Source: *Financial Times* 24 December 1987

Figure 4.1
It may be difficult to determine from data whether the external value of a currency has been 'rising' or 'falling' in value. The external value of the pound sterling can be measured against other individual currencies, and against baskets of other currencies. The apparent strength of the pound against the dollar, for example, may just be an indication of the weakness of the dollar. To get a good idea of the strength of a currency it is necessary to look at the value using a number of different exchange rates.

1. Did the pound sterling strengthen or weaken against all other currencies and baskets of currencies between (a) 1983 and 1984, and (b) 1986 and 1987? Explain your answer.

2. Calculate whether the dollar strengthened or weakened against the yen between December 1983 and April 1988.

Figure 4.2
Economic events are being analysed increasingly from an international perspective. Serious newspapers are less and less likely to view economic events, such as interest rate and exchange rate movements, solely from the British perspective. Increasingly over recent years, economies have become interdependent, mainly because of the growth of world trade and improvements in communications. Events in the British economy are therefore progressively bound up with changes in the economies of countries like the USA and Japan, and this is reflected in newspaper reports.

3. (a) Which country's central bank is given as much prominence as the Bank of England in the article? (b) Why should this newspaper give front page prominence to the actions of another country's central bank?

Figure 4.3
Countries are frequently grouped together for the purposes of international economic co-operation, or just for the purpose of economic analysis. Nations often group together to achieve some common purpose. The European Community, for example, is a group of nations whose primary aim is to create a common market between them. Nations are sometimes grouped together by economists simply for the purpose of economic analysis. For example, the UK is classed as a 'developed' nation for the purpose of economic analysis although there is no official organisation of nations called 'The Developed Nations'. Other groupings formed for a similar purpose would include the oil-producing nations and the newly industrialised countries.

4. Is G7 a number of countries grouped together just for the purposes of economic analysis? Explain your answer.

APPLYING ECONOMIC PRINCIPLES

1. (a) Define (i) the Effective Sterling Exchange Rate (ii) ECU, and (iii) SDR. (b) (i) Refer to the other exchange rates shown in Figure 4.1 and explain why the Sterling Effective Exchange Rate rose between 1984 and 1985, while sterling against the ECU fell in the same period. (ii) What economic factors could have accounted for these changes?

2. (a) Explain the relationship between interest rates and exchange rates. (b) Refer to Figure 4.2. (i) What happened to UK interest rates and West German interest rates at the beginning of 1985? (ii) What factors could have accounted for your answer? (c) Explain the policies of the central banks in late 1987, referred to in Figure 4.2.

3. (a) Refer to Figure 4.2. What was the Louvre Accord of February 1987? (b) Why did the Louvre Accord suggest that the dollar should be stabilised at its February 1987 value? (c) Why did the G7 need to reaffirm their desire for stable exchange rates? (d) Why was there no commitment to a specific value for the dollar by the end of 1987, in spite of the Louvre Accord?

4. (a) Use a supply and demand diagram to show why the external value of the dollar fell as a result of its external deficit in 1987. (b) On another diagram show how intervention by central banks could increase the exchange rate of the dollar. (c) What forms could such intervention take?

5. (a) Explain the circumstances under which the supply curve for a currency could slope (i) upwards and to the right, and (ii) downwards and to the right. (b) (i) Draw a supply and demand diagram for a currency. The supply curve for the currency should slope downwards and to the right with a less steep slope than the demand curve for the currency. (ii) Show on the diagram, and explain, what would happen if there was a drop in demand for the country's exports.

FOR FURTHER INVESTIGATION
Exchange rate movements are widely quoted in quality newspapers. Study these and, on a graph, record movements of sterling against the dollar, the deutschmark and the yen over a period of several months. Annotate the graph to indicate the reasons for major changes in the movements of currencies. Write a short report describing and explaining the changes shown on your graph.

ESSAYS
Refer to the data wherever possible, especially in the first essay.
1. (a) Describe the major changes in exchange rates during the 1980s. (b) Why do governments often intervene in the foreign exchange markets? What forms has this intervention taken?
2. (a) How might the United Kingdom Government bring about a rise in sterling's exchange rate? (b) What might be the consequences of such a rise? [SUJB 6/85]

Ins and outs

Figure 5.1
The UK balance of payments

£ million	1975	1985
Current account		
Visible trade		
Exports (fob)	19 330	78 051
Imports (fob)	-22 663	-80 162
Visible balance	-3 333	-2 111
Invisibles		
Credits	14 999	80 608
Debits	-13 248	-74 895
Invisibles balance	1 751	5 713
of which:		
Services balance	1 336	5 812
Interest, profits and dividends balance	890	3 400
Transfers balance	-475	-3 499
Current balance	-1 582	3 602
Transactions in external assets and liabilities[1]		
Investment overseas by UK residents		
Direct	-1 324	-7 307
Portfolio	-59	-18 220
Total UK investment overseas	-1 383	-25 527
Investment in the United Kingdom by overseas residents		
Direct	1 518	3 370
Portfolio	194	7 065
Total overseas investment in the United Kingdom	1 712	10 435

£ million	1975	1985
Foreign currency lending abroad by UK banks[2]		-20 286
Foreign currency borrowing abroad by UK banks[2]	545	25 402
Net foreign currency transactions of UK banks	545	5 116
	-184	-1 573
Sterling lending abroad by UK banks		
Sterling borrowing and deposit liabilities abroad of UK banks	305	4 171
Net sterling transactions of UK banks	121	2 598
Deposits with and lending to banks abroad by UK non-bank private sector		-3 760
Borrowing from banks abroad by:		
UK non-bank private sector	282	2 283
Public corporations	299	64
General government	100	87
Official reserves (additions to - /drawings on +)	655	-1 758
Other external assets of:		
UK non-bank private sector and public corporations	-1	3 613
General government	-621	-730
Other external liabilities of:		
UK non-bank private sector and public corporations	322	343
General government	-430	-60
Net transactions in assets and liabilities	1 601	-7 296
Allocation of special drawing rights	—	—
Balancing item	-19	3 694

1. Assets: increase - /decrease +. Liabilities: increase + /decrease -

Source: *Annual Abstract of Statistics.*

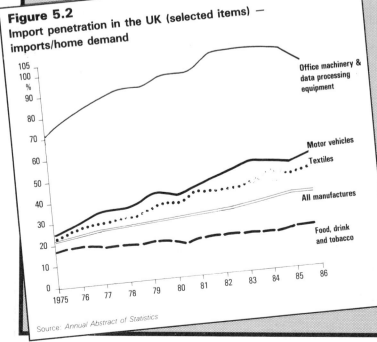

Figure 5.2
Import penetration in the UK (selected items) — imports/home demand

Office machinery & data processing equipment

Motor vehicles

Textiles

All manufactures

Food, drink and tobacco

Source: *Annual Abstract of Statistics*

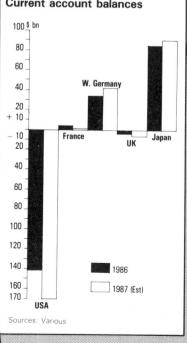

Figure 5.3
Current account balances

$ bn

W. Germany

France

UK

Japan

USA

■ 1986
□ 1987 (Est)

Sources: Various

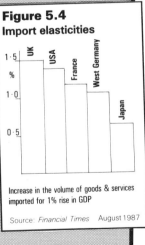

Figure 5.4
Import elasticities

UK USA France West Germany Japan

Increase in the volume of goods & services imported for 1% rise in GDP

Source: *Financial Times*   August 1987

Figure 5.1

It is important to distinguish the most significant information in complex data or statistics. Economic data appear frequently in very complex forms; and sometimes it is the sheer volume of data which can appear confusing. Government statistics in particular may contain a mass of information; but economists may be interested only in selected portions for the purpose of analysis. It is important to study headings and subheadings carefully to decide what information is required for a particular purpose. Frequently only a very small percentage of data will be relevant to a particular task.

1. Which section of the balance of payments is relevant to someone interested in the UK trade in goods?

2. The balance of payments always balances. Which two figures balance exactly the 'Net transactions in assets and liabilities'?

Figure 5.2

The significance of an economic indicator may be recognized only when it is compared to other indicators. Statistics often have little significance in themselves, and they may need to be compared to some other statistics to have any meaning. For example, a country's growth rate may look impressive in isolation, but it can be seen in perspective only if compared to the country's own growth rate in the past, or to the growth rate of other nations.

3. In what sense may UK import penetration of textiles in 1985 be regarded as (a) 'low' and (b) 'high'?

4. What other information would help you to assess whether the UK has a generally 'high' import penetration?

Figure 5.3

Care must be taken when inferring trends from limited data. Economists and politicians need to identify trends from statistics to enable them to predict for the future. Without such predictions it would be impossible to prepare and implement policies. However, it may be difficult for a number of reasons to identify trends. For example, only a limited time period may be given, and some trends may be discernible only over decades. There is also the problem that some statistics change in a far less predictable way than others: for example, it is much easier to predict future trends in population than in share prices.

5. Can it be inferred from the data that the UK's current account deficit was worsening in the late 1980s? Explain your answer.

6. Which would you expect to be more unpredictable over a three-year period: (a) balance of payments current accounts, or (b) exchange rates? Explain your answer.

Figure 5.4

'Elasticity' does not always refer to price elasticity of demand. The word 'elasticity' refers to the responsiveness of changes in one variable to changes in another. There are many types of elasticity, including price elasticity of supply and cross elasticity of demand. When elasticity is mentioned in articles and in statistics it is often price elasticity of demand that is being referred to, though it should not be assumed that this is always the case.

7. What type of elasticity is being referred to in the bar chart? Give reasons for your answer.

APPLYING ECONOMIC PRINCIPLES

1. With reference to Figure 5.1: (a) Can it be inferred that the volume of imports increased approximately fourfold between 1975 and 1985? Explain your answer. (b) What was the size of the visible deficit in (i) 1975, and (ii) 1985? (iii) Explain why the government would have been far more concerned about the visible deficit in 1975 than in 1985. (c) What was the value of UK investment overseas in (i) 1975 and (ii) 1985? (iii) What were the possible costs and benefits to the UK of the 1985 figure? (d) What happened to reserves in (i) 1975 and (ii) 1985? (iii) Give possible reasons for these figures.

2. Refer to Figure 5.4 (a) For which countries in the data is the demand for imports elastic in relation to national income? Explain your answer. (b) For what reasons might Japan have a relatively low income elasticity of demand for imports? (c) What policies might be adopted to reduce the UK's income elasticity of demand for imports?

3. (a) What do Figures 5.2 and 5.4 suggest about the competitiveness of: (i) UK manufacturing industries, and (ii) the UK economy as a whole? Support your answer with appropriate data. (b) What factors might explain the levels of UK competitiveness identified in (a)? (c) What other information, apart from Figures 5.2 and 5.4, would enable you to make a more accurate assessment of UK competitiveness?

4. (a) Identify the main components of the UK balance of payments. (b) What factors might cause the UK balance of payments current account to vary? Illustrate your answer with reference to recent UK experience. (c) What impact would you expect the situation shown on Figure 5.3 to have on the world economy? Explain your answer.

FOR FURTHER INVESTIGATION

Balance of payments figures are widely reported each month in the media, not only for the UK but also for other major industrialized economies like the USA and Japan. There is a connection between the balance of payments performance of the major nations. Collect information about the balance of payments for the UK, USA and one other major industrialized nation. Write a report analysing the statistics you have collected. Concentrate on the trade balance, which is more widely reported than the invisible balance. Outline the reasons for the patterns and trends that you have discovered, and explain how the balance of payments performance of one country affects the performance of others.

ESSAYS

Refer to the data wherever possible, especially in the first essay.

1. Explain why the UK will be so reliant on its invisible exports in future years.

2. Why might a government wish to eliminate a surplus on its current account balance of payments? What measures could it use to achieve this end? [London 6/87]

Mountains and lakes

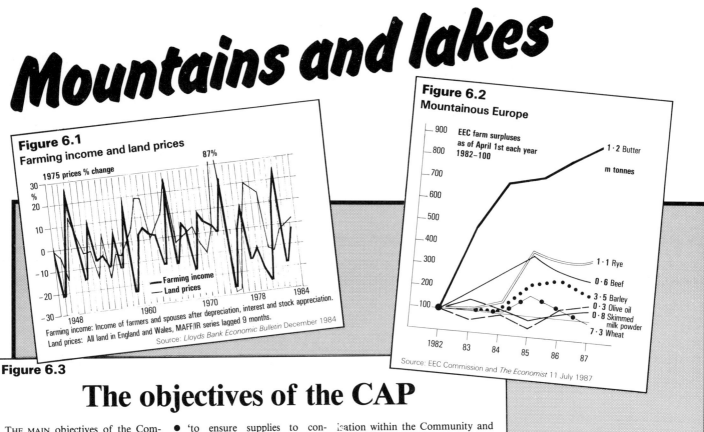

Figure 6.1
Farming income and land prices

1975 prices % change

Farming income: Income of farmers and spouses after depreciation, interest and stock appreciation, MAFF/IR series lagged 9 months.
Land prices: All land in England and Wales.
Source: *Lloyds Bank Economic Bulletin* December 1984

Figure 6.2
Mountainous Europe

EEC farm surpluses
as of April 1st each year
1982=100

1·2 Butter
m tonnes
1·1 Rye
0·6 Beef
3·5 Barley
0·3 Olive oil
0·8 Skimmed milk powder
7·3 Wheat

Source: EEC Commission and *The Economist* 11 July 1987

Figure 6.3

The objectives of the CAP

THE MAIN objectives of the Common Agricultural Policy of the EC are:

● 'to increase agricultural productivity by promoting technical progress and by ensuring the rational development of agricultural production and the optimum utilisation of all factors of production, in particular labour';

● to ensure thereby 'a fair standard of living for the agricultural community, in particular by increasing the individual earnings of persons engaged in agriculture';

● 'to stabilise markets';

● 'to provide certainty of supplies';

● 'to ensure supplies to consumers at reasonable prices'.

The final objectives of the CAP were established after the Stresa Conference in 1958 which was convened in accordance with the Treaty. The additional objectives were in the spirit of the Treaty:

● to increase farm incomes not only by a system of transfers from the non-farm population through a price support policy but also by the encouragement of rural industrialisation to give alternative opportunities to farm labour;

● to contribute to overall economic growth by allowing special-isation within the Community and eliminating artificial market distortions;

● to preserve the family farm and to ensure that structural and price policies go hand in hand.

It can be seen, therefore, that the CAP was not preoccupied simply with the implementation of common prices and market supports; it also included a commitment to encourage the structural improvement of farming. However, the EC expenditure on the structural aspects of the CAP remains very small indeed (less than 6% of total CAP expenditure).

Source: *The Economic Review* September 1984 (based on Article 39 of the Treaty of Rome)

Figure 6.4

Reforming the CAP

THE GREEN PAPER puts forward options for fundamental reform of the CAP, taking into account national and international factors. The consequences of these options are likely to be restraints on production, more effective pricing policies, and shifts in rural populations. The outlook for the success of the proposals is not good. The Commission has been trying since 1980 to convince agricultural ministers of the dangerous implications for the future of their policies and failure to take action. The crux of the problem is cereal production. There seems to be the choice available of a drastic cutting of cereal prices in real terms, or of introducing extra methods of management of supply. In seven of the EEC countries over 50 per cent of farmers grow cereals. Some specialist arable farmers have created large, efficient businesses and could survive cuts in price guarantees. Most of the rest would be seriously affected.

Against this, however, there is the spectre of ever-growing surpluses. Output of cereals averaged 125 million tonnes from 1980-3. In 1984 the harvest was 155 million tonnes and this figure is expected to become the norm if no action is taken. The options available include the creation of a cereals board to control acreages planted and to administer a new structure of quotas, deficiency payments, and price guarantee thresholds. This might be linked to payments to farmers to leave their land fallow or to use it for other crops such as timber, oilseed, fruit, or, in some areas, cotton. Some products with industrial uses might be substituted. The starch from sugar beet and potatoes might, for example, be used in paper and cardboard manufacture. Similar proposals have been made for dealing with butter surpluses by concentrating the butter as a cooking fat or by feeding it in an adapted form to cattle. The other major option for cereals is to adjust the support prices more closely in line with international price movements. The CAP has had the effect of isolating the EEC producers from these international price movements. Hence the price gap between internal EEC and world markets has widened and the result is an increase in the cost to the Community budget of export restitution payments.

Source: *British Economy Survey* Spring 1986 (based on the EC's Green paper on the Future of the CAP July 1985)

Figure 6.1
Where variables appear to be related, it may be difficult to infer causality. A major task for economists is to analyse how variables are related. Sometimes economists cannot agree on the direction of causality — that is if two variable are moving in the same direction it is not always clear which one is causing the other to change, or whether both are in fact responding to some third variable. For example, economists often argue about whether changes in the money supply cause changes in the rate of inflation, or vice-versa: both might be linked to some third variable, such as the national income.

1. In what ways might farming income and land prices be related?

2. (**a**) Do the data suggest that farm income is the main determinant of farmland prices? (**b**) What other information might help you to assess the relationship?

Figure 6.2
Variables moving in different directions may make the identification of trends difficult. Economists try to identify patterns and trends in data in order to make better policy decisions. A problem arises when figures are moving in different directions. The picture might be further complicated by the fact that some figures are more significant than others. For example, a very large increase in the price of shoes might have little effect on the Retail Prices Index which measures the rate of inflation; any change in the price of food, however, will have a significant effect on the Retail Prices Index.

3. Which farm product made the largest contribution to EEC farm surpluses in 1987?

4. Why is it difficult to identify an overall trend in farm surpluses?

Figure 6.3
Apparently precise statements of government policy or legislation may contain ambiguities. When governments pass legislation they try to be very precise in the meaning of the terms that they use. This is to help people who have to put laws into practice, and to help judges if they are required to sort out disputes about the law. Sometimes it is very difficult to sort out what a piece of legislation means: for example, competition law has rested on the basis that takeovers and mergers should be 'in the public interest', but in practice it is very difficult to determine precisely what this phrase means.

5. Write down two phrases mentioned here that are difficult to define precisely in economic terms.

Figure 6.4
It may be difficult to identify the main points in a detailed piece of data. Some data contain a great deal of information, much of it giving a very detailed analysis of the subject under consideration. In documentary data, such as newspapers and magazine articles, it is necessary to establish the main point that is being made in each paragraph before getting involved in the details of the paragraph. Sometimes, but not always, the opening sentence will outline the theme of that paragraph.

6. The first paragraph identifies some of the proposals for reform of the Common Agricultural Policy, and some problems involved with such reform. What main points are made in the second paragraph?

APPLYING ECONOMIC PRINCIPLES

1. Refer to Figure 6.1.
(**a**) What is meant by 'agricultural productivity'? (**b**) Explain how agricultural productivity can be increased by (**i**) 'technical progress', and (**ii**) 'encouraging ... rural industrialization to give alternative opportunities to farm labour'.

2. Refer to Figure 6.3.
(**a**) What is meant by the aim 'to stabilize markets'? To what extent has this aim been realized by the Common Agriculture Policy? Use data from Figures 6.1 and 6.2 to support your answer. (**b**) What is meant by the 'structural improvement of farming'? How can this be improved by larger farms?

3. (**a**) Why do many agricultural products have price inelastic demand? (**b**) Use a supply and demand diagram to show that price inelastic demand coupled with erratic supply can lead to fluctuations in the incomes of farmers, as shown in Figure 6.1.

4. Many farm products might have very low positive, or even negative, income elasticity of demand. (**a**) Explain the term 'low positive income elasticity of demand'. (**b**) What name is given to goods with negative income elasticity of demand? (**c**) Why have many agricultural products got low income elasticity of demand? (**d**) What problem is caused to the farming industry by low income elasticities of demand? Explain how this problem arises and give evidence from Figure 6.2.

5. Use an example from Figure 6.2 to show, by a supply and demand diagram, how the imposition of an intervention price by the EC above the market price of an agricultural product will lead to a surplus. Indicate the revenue that farmers would receive (**a**) without EC intervention, and (**b**) with EC intervention.

FOR FURTHER INVESTIGATION
The *Annual Abstract of Statistics*, available at all main reference libraries, carries details of agricultural output at constant prices. Draw two pie charts, one for the most recent year available, and one for ten years previously. The pie charts should represent total output, and their respective sizes should indicate the increase in the value of output at constant prices over the ten-year period. Divide each chart into the four main areas of agricultural output (crops, horticulture, livestock and livestock products), in proportion to their relative importance. Write a summary paragraph which indicates the extent of the increase in farm output, and the extent to which individual products are contributing to the increase. Quote figures in your answer. Indicate what problems your findings could pose for the operation of the Common Agricultural Policy

ESSAYS
Refer to the data wherever possible, especially in the first essay.

1. What are the main aims of the Common Agricultural Policy of the EC? Describe how the CAP operates, and what problems are encountered with the policy.

2. Why and how do governments intervene to regulate the prices of agricultural commodites? [London 6/86]

Black gold

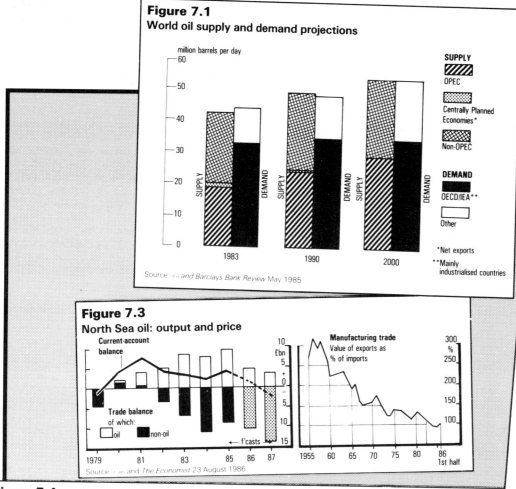

Figure 7.1
World oil supply and demand projections

million barrels per day

SUPPLY
OPEC
Centrally Planned Economies*
Non-OPEC

DEMAND
OECD/IEA**
Other

1983   1990   2000

*Net exports
**Mainly industrialised countries

Source: and Barclays Bank Review May 1985

Figure 7.2
Oil and the UK economy

price $ per barrel

production m tonnes

1975 77 79 81 83 85 87

1986 and 1987 figures are estimates
Source: The Economist 21 February 1987

Figure 7.3
North Sea oil: output and price

Current-account balance
£bn
Trade balance
of which:
oil   non-oil
← f'casts

1979 81 83 85 86 87

Manufacturing trade
Value of exports as % of imports
%

1955 60 65 70 75 80 86 1st half

Source: and The Economist 23 August 1986

Figure 7.4

OPEC humbled with the dollar

The real price of oil varies from country to country because of currency changes and local inflation rates. In February 1985, when the dollar was at its peak and oil cost $28 a barrel, Japan paid Y7,200 a barrel. By July 1986, the dollar price of oil had tumbled by 65% to less than $10 a barrel, but the yen price had fallen even further because of the dollar's slide—to Y1,500 a barrel. Allowing for Japan's modest inflation rate, the real price it paid for its oil fell altogether by 79% between February 1985 and July last year.

European countries did almost as well. Result: euphoria in all big industrial countries, except in oil-exporting Britain.

The dollar's continuing slide since last July means that OPEC's efforts to lift the oil price since mid-1986 have had little effect on many consuming countries' oil import bills. After allowing for its domestic inflation, the real price now paid by Japan is Y2,600 a barrel—Y1,100 more than it paid in July last year, but still 64% less than in February 1985.

The four big European economies are only slightly worse off. Britain still has the least to cheer about—its exported barrels are now worth 60% less than they were when the dollar peaked.

The United States, unsheltered by the dollar's decline, is now paying 37% less than it did in February 1985 for imported oil, but nearly twice as much as a year ago. Newly-industrialised countries such as South Korea, whose currencies have moved with the dollar, have fared much the same. Some Latin American countries, with currencies depreciating even faster than the dollar, have seen their real oil import bills rise fastest. But Mexico, exporting some 1.3m barrels a day, has seen the real peso value of each barrel rise nearly 2½ times since last July.

The negligible increase in most countries' real oil prices over the past year ought to have kept demand buoyant. But, while last year saw world oil demand rise by 2.2%, the International Energy Agency (IEA) reckons that consumption will increase by only 1% in 1987. With economic growth faltering almost everywhere, such estimates will probably be revised downwards later this year. That slack demand should help deter OPEC from raising prices when it next meets on June 25th.

Source: The Economist 13 June 1987

Figure 7.1

It may be more difficult to predict some trends than others. Economists need to make predictions about future trends in order to make economic planning and policy more accurate. It is far easier, however, to predict certain trends than others. For example, it might be relatively easy to predict with some accuracy the *demand* for an agricultural product in an economy for a five-year period; but the *supply* of the product might be subject to large fluctuations because of changes in the weather.

1. What are the principal factors affecting (**a**) the world supply of oil, and (**b**) the world demand for oil?

2. Which is likely to be the more reliable, and why — the prediction about oil supplies or the prediction about oil demand?

Figure 7.2

A change in the price of oil in one currency does not necessarily mean an equivalent rise in the price of oil in another currency. Oil is traded mainly in dollars. A rise in the dollar price of oil might lead to a fall in the exchange rate of the dollar against the pound. In this case, the percentage increase in the dollar price of oil will be greater than the percentage increase in the price paid for oil in sterling.

3. What was the approximate fall in the dollar price of oil, both in dollars and in percentage terms, between 1984 and 1986?

4. If the pound sterling was worth $1.16 in 1984 and $1.48 in 1986, what was the approximate fall in the sterling price of oil, both in pounds and in percentage terms, between 1984 and 1986?

Figure 7.3

Apparently favourable economic statistics can mask unfavourable underlying trends. Favourable economic indicators must sometimes be treated with caution because they may mask worrying underlying trends. For example, in the 1950s the British economy grew very strongly; however the encouraging figures masked other worrying long-term trends such as a poor investment rate in the UK. Unfavourable underlying trends are not necessarily permanent, however, as economic circumstances constantly change.

5. What favourable economic situation is shown on the left-hand graph between 1980 and 1985, and what unfavourable situation underlay it?

6. Can it be inferred from the data that the current account of the balance of payments is destined to fall into permanent deficit in the 1990s? Explain your answer.

Figure 7.4

The language used in newspaper and magazine articles might exaggerate for the purpose of emphasis. Newspaper and magazine articles often use words like 'massive', 'dramatic', 'devastating' and 'crash' to describe economic events. These words can be used to emphasize strongly a particular viewpoint, or to make an article more lively and interesting. However, a tendency to exaggerate may be misleading.

7. Identify two words in the passage that could be said to over-emphasize the particular point being made, and explain the same points in more moderate language.

APPLYING ECONOMIC PRINCIPLES

1. With reference to Figure 7.1 (**a**) Were world oil prices expected to rise or fall in 1990? Explain your answer. (**b**) The Soviet Union is the world's second largest producer of oil. What factors could account for the fact that the supply of oil from centrally planned economies is such a small, and declining, part of 'world' oil supply? (**c**) What will be the likely effect on the world oil market in future if the Soviet Union becomes a net importer of oil?

2. (**a**) What does Figure 7.2 suggest about the price elasticity of supply for oil? Explain your answer. (**b**) Using the prices from Figure 7.2 draw supply and demand diagrams to show what happened to the market for oil (assuming North Sea oil prices reflect oil prices generally): (**i**) between 1979 and 1981, when disturbances in the Middle East restricted world oil supplies; (**ii**) between 1985 and 1986 when the OPEC agreement to limit output broke down.

3. With reference to Figure 7.3: (**a**) Define: (**i**) the current account balance; (**ii**) the trade balance; and (**iii**) the non-oil trade balance. (**b**) Describe the trends in the UK balance of payments between 1979 and 1987. (**c**) Explain the importance of the oil balance to the UK economy over this period. (**d**) Refer to Figures 7.2 and 7.3 and (**i**) describe what was expected to happen to the oil balance after 1985. Give a reason for your answer. (**ii**) What problem might this have been expected to cause for the UK balance of payments in the 1990s? (**e**) (**i**) What effect would North Sea oil have had on the exchange rate of the pound in the early 1980s? (**ii**) Explain the effect that the exchange rate movement would have had on the sale of other visible exports for this period. (**f**) What benefits could be gained for the UK economy from a decline in the production of North Sea oil? How would this affect your answer to 3 (**d**) (**ii**).

4. With reference to Figure 7.4: (**a**) Define 'the real ..price of oil'. (**b**) Explain why the price paid for oil by Japan fell faster in percentage terms between February 1985 and July 1986 than the price paid by the USA. (**c**) Describe the possible effects of a substantial fall in oil prices for (**i**) nations who consume but do not produce oil, and (**ii**) for the UK.

FOR FURTHER INVESTIGATION

Oil supplies are unreliable and non-renewable, and a great deal of pollution is associated with the use of oil. Try to find some information on other sources of energy. Construct a large grid. Down the side list the energy sources. Have columns for private costs, private benefits, external costs and external benefits. Write summary notes in each of the boxes defined by the grid. Write a brief report, giving reasons, about whether you think power stations should ideally use oil, coal or nuclear energy.

ESSAYS

Refer to the data wherever possible, especially in the first essay.

1. What factors affect the price of oil in (**a**) the short term, and (**b**) the longer term?

2. Can market forces be relied upon to balance the prospective decline in North Sea oil production by adequate expansion in other sectors? [London 6/87]

A material world

Figure 8.1
Living standards over 30 years

	1957(†)	1987(†)
% of household owning a:		
house	33	63
car	24	61
TV	66	97
washing machine	34	82
fridge	15	98
inside bathroom and/or hot water system	75	96
% of average household expenditure on:		
housing	9	20
food	33	20
number of:		
people taking trips abroad	2 million	16 million
trade union members	8.3 million	9.6 million
+ 18s in full-time education	200 000	600 000
children in fee-paying independent schools	250 000	450 000
national daily newspaper sales	16.8 million	15.1 million
number of books published	1 000	8 000
total attendances at League soccer matches	33.6 million	16.5 million
beer consumed per person per year	150 pints	190 pints
wine consumed per person per year	1.1 litres	11 litres
spirits consumed per person per year	0.5 litre	1.5 litres

(†) Where it has not been possible to use exact figures from 1957 and 1987, we have used sources from the nearest possible year.

Source: *Which?* March 1987

Figure 8.2
Gross Domestic Product in 1985

Country	£ billion* GDP	Country	£* GDP per head
US	2250	US	9400
Japan	800	Canada	8500
West Germany	425	Norway	8000
France	355	Luxembourg	7800
UK	**350**	Sweden	7200
Italy	305	Denmark	7000
Canada	215	West Germany	6900
Spain	170	Japan	6600
Netherlands	95	Finland	6500
Belgium	60	France	6500
Sweden	60	Netherlands	6500
Austria	45	**UK**	**6200**
Denmark	35	Belgium	6100
Greece	35	Austria	6000
Norway	35	Italy	5400
Finland	30	Spain	4400
Portugal	30	Ireland	4000
Ireland	15	Greece	3400
Luxembourg	5	Portugal	3000

*Converted to sterling using PPPs.

Source: OECD/Eurostat and *Economic Progress Report* (Treasury), 1987

PPPs = Purchasing Power Parities. If market exchange rates are used to convert other countries GDP to pounds sterling, differences in price levels between different nations could be ignored. Converting GDP to PPPs gives a better indication of the purchasing power of a given level of GDP in different countries.

Figure 8.3
International living standards

(GDP per head on percentage of EEC-12 average, using PPPs)

	1960	1965	1970	1975	1980	1985
US	188	182	162.8	153.6	150.8	157
Japan	56.5	71.3	93.3	94.9	101.7	112.3
France	101.6	103.6	106	110.4	111.6	108.9
Germany	114.67	116.9	113.7	109.7	114.4	116.1
Italy	91.6	93.8	100.8	97.6	102	103.1
UK	128.5	119.1	107.9	105.6	100.7	103.9

Source: Eurostat and *Guardian* 26 August 1987

PPPs = Purchasing Power Parities. If market exchange rates are used to convert other countries GDP to pounds sterling, differences in price levels between different nations could be ignored. Converting GDP to PPPs gives a better indication of the purchasing power of a given level of GDP in different countries.

Figure 8.4

Reports paint portrait of despair

A DEVASTATING portrait of an impoverished, illiterate, untrained Britain, in which true unemployment is much worse than official estimates but executive pay is still expanding at double the rate of inflation, emerges from reports published today.

● Nearly one in three UK taxpayers has an income below the Council of Europe's decency threshold, with 6.5 million on less than £125 a week, according to the Low Pay Unit.

● About a quarter of those entering the job training scheme (JTS) for young adult long-term jobless are illiterate, according to a Manpower Services Commission-backed training agency.

● Official government figures underestimate the true level of unemployment by nearly 50 per cent, according to Dr Fred Robinson of Newcastle University who has identified a "jobs gap" of 4.7 million.

● Sexual stereotyping and discrimination is rampant in new training schemes, according to the TUC, and these schemes are creating waste and despair according to Apex Trust, a charity for ex-offenders.

● Executives in the quarter to January got average annual increases of 7.5 per cent, with some getting as high as 30 per cent and exceptional individuals generally getting between 12 and 15 per cent, according to Incomes Data Services.

The Low Pay Unit, in a report on the eve of next week's budget, Two Nations — Double Standards, says that out of £8.1 billion given away in tax cuts since 1979 the poorest six million taxpayers have got only 8 per cent. The richest million taxpayers — 5 per cent of the total — have shared between them one third of the total tax cuts.

It says Mrs Thatcher's boast that taxpayers have enjoyed an average tax cut of £7 a week ignores the fact that most of this went to the better off so that one on £70,000 a year has gained £367 a week while the low paid have got less than £2 a week offset by increased indirect taxes.

The unit argues that, far from easing the poverty trap, government policy has increased the number of poor families in it fivefold: from 90,000 in 1979 to half a million today.

Mr Peter Davison of the Kedder Training Agency says the 25 per cent rate of illiteracy found in JTS entrants is an improvement on earlier figures as high as 35 per cent but adds that the majority entering the scheme have no qualifications at all.

"When we first started last November we had to arrange courses for these people at local colleges which made reading and writing part of their training programme," he says.

Source: David Gow, *Guardian* 7 March 1987

Figure 8.1
Some variables may be difficult to measure and other data may be used to indicate changes in them. Some economic variables may be fairly straightforward to define and measure: for example, visible exports. Others are both difficult to define and/or difficult to measure: for example, 'economic development'. In such cases, a number of other indicators may be used to try and measure the variable in question. Literacy rates, for example, might be used as an indicator of the economic development of a developing nation.

1. What is meant by 'the standard of living'?
2. Explain how a decline in the percentage of household income spent on food can be an indicator of rising living standards.

Figure 8.2
Living standards are not the same as general welfare. The standard of living refers to the material living standards of the average person in a country. General welfare is even more difficult to define and measure: it may be taken to refer to the general happiness and well-being of the population. Most people would accept that it is difficult to be happy if living standards are very low; however, it does not automatically follow that happiness increases proportionately with increases in material living standards. For this, and other reasons, figures giving measures of living standards must be treated with caution.

3. (a) Describe the GDP per head of the Irish compared to that of the West Germans. (b) In the mid-1980s a survey suggested that the Irish were the happiest people in Europe. Give two factors, other than material living standards, that might cause the average citizen in Ireland to be happier than the average citizen in West Germany.

4. The US spends far more per head on weapons than the West Germans. How might this affect the interpretation of the tables?

Figures 8.2 and 8.3
Account must be taken of purchasing power differences when comparing living standards between countries. Living standards are affected by the price that people have to pay for goods in the shops. To say that someone earns more in one country than another—even allowing for problems in comparing earnings in different currencies—is not to say that they have more purchasing power. Figures showing GDP will sometimes be statistically adjusted to allow for this problem.

5. Why have the figures in the tables been converted to PPPs?
6. What does the figure of '157' for the US in Figure 8.3 mean?

Figure 8.4
The way statistics are presented may give emphasis to a particular point. Economists and politicians may use different statistics to defend different points of view on a subject, and they may even argue over the interpretation of the same set of statistics. For example, in 1988 the government reformed social security. The government, in defending the changes, kept emphasizing the percentage who would gain or who were no worse off, whilst opponents kept emphasizing the percentage that would lose out.

7. How could the statistic related to the job training scheme be reinterpreted to give emphasis to the literacy of trainees?

APPLYING ECONOMIC PRINCIPLES

1. (a) Select **two** items in Figure 8.1 that you think are good indicators of living standards and explain why you think they are good measures. (b) Suggest **two** other possible indicators of standards of living not mentioned in Figure 8.1. Explain your answer. (c) Economic theory assumes that consumers are rational utility maximizers, and that increased consumption always increases consumers' welfare. Why might these assumptions be invalid? Use examples from the data in your explanation where appropriate.

2. (a) What are 'inferior goods'? (b) Refer to Figure 8.1 and suggest which items in the data might be inferior goods. Give reasons to explain why they might be inferior goods.

3. (a) What do Figures 8.2 and 8.3 suggest about living standards in the UK in relation to other countries? (b) What problems are involved in using GDP as an indicator of living standards?

4. (a) What indicators of general welfare are suggested by the article in Figure 8.4? (b) What conclusions does the writer reach concerning the distribution of income in the UK? Support your answer with evidence from the article. (c) Why is the distribution of income relevant to the estimation of a country's standard of living?

5. For most consumer durable goods there has been increasing supply and increasing demand over recent years: (a) List the factors that have led both to an increase in demand and an increase in supply for consumer durable goods. (b) Draw a diagram to show the likely effects of this increasing supply and demand on the quantities of consumer durables traded, and their price.

6. (a) What are 'economic bads'? (b) What other economic term could be used to describe economic bads? (c) With reference to economic bads, explain how a rise in living standards could be accompanied by a reduction in general welfare.

FOR FURTHER INVESTIGATION
Each generation benefits or suffers from the development of new products. Undertake a survey to find out some of the consumer durable goods that were not available to your grandparents' generation, but were available to your parents' generation. Find out some of the consumer durable goods that have only recently become available. Write a report incorporating your findings and assessing the social costs and benefits of an increasing number of consumer durable goods.

ESSAYS
Refer to the data wherever possible, especially in the first essay.

1. To what extent can the UK be said to have been enjoying increasing living standards in recent years?
2. Evaluate the competing claims of the following measures to be indicators of a country's standard of living: (a) GNP at factor cost per head; (b) consumers' expenditure per head; (c) the stock of durable goods held by consumers. [Oxford 6/85]

9 Saving

For a rainy day

Figure 9.1
Savings, consumption and real incomes

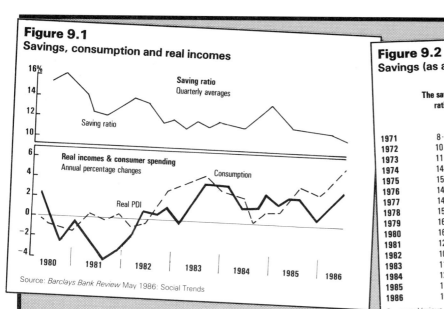

Saving ratio
Quarterly averages

Saving ratio

Real incomes & consumer spending
Annual percentage changes

Consumption

Real PDI

Source: *Barclays Bank Review* May 1986: Social Trends

Figure 9.2
Savings (as a % of PDI)

	The savings ratio	Inflation (Annual % rate)	Bank base rate (Highest During year — %)	Investment ratio (GDFCF as a % of GDP)
1971	8·5	9·4	5	21·0
1972	10·5	7·1	7½	21·0
1973	11·7	9·2	13	22·3
1974	14·1	19·1	12½	22·0
1975	15·4	24·9	11½	21·9
1976	14·9	15·1	14	21·5
1977	14·5	12·1	13	20·9
1978	15·0	8·4	12½	21·5
1979	16·5	13·4	17	20·9
1980	16·0	18·0	16	20·9
1981	12·5	11·9	16	19·1
1982	10·5	8·6	14	19·0
1983	11·6	4·6	11	19·0
1984	12·3	5·0	12	20·2
1985	11·3	6·1	14	19·9
1986	10·6	3·4	12½	19·7

Sources: Various

Figure 9.3
Personal sector financial assets (end 1984)

	Amount £m	Percentage of total
Notes and coin	10 010	1.8
Short term assets		
Sight deposits at banks	25 600	4.5
Other deposits at banks	33 372	5.9
National Savings Bank deposits	6 553	1.2
Building society deposits	90 492	15.9
Other	437	0.1
Long term assets		
National Savings Certificates/Bonds	19 805	3.5
Premium Bonds	1 742	0.3
British government securities	18 400	3.2
Stocks and shares	81 400	14.3
Unit trusts	8 474	1.5
Overseas assets	10 261	1.8
Trade and other debtors	26 000	4.6
Other	6 754	1.2
Equity in life assurance and pension funds	227 250	39.9
Accrued interest, tax etc	3 063	0.5
Total	569 613	100.0

Note. Some of the figures are approximate, and have been rounded.

Source: Association of British Insurers *Money Management Review* Spring 1987

Figure 9.4
Savings in different counties

Household savings ratios
As % of personal disposable income

☐ 1983 ▨ 1984
▨ 1985 ■ 1986 est

United States   Britain   Canada   France   W. Germany   Japan   Italy

Source: IMF and *The Economist* 9 May 1987

Figure 9.1
Changes can be expressed over different time periods.
Changes in variables may be measured over different time periods as, for example, 'annual percentage changes', 'quarterly averages', 'monthly averages' etc. Some economic indicators are measured over different time periods. For example, a rise in retail prices can be shown as the percentage increase in the price of a basket of goods over the same month the previous year. It can also be expressed as an index number, relating the current price of a basket of goods to the price on a base date.

1. Explain what is meant by a 'quarterly average' for the savings ratio figure. Use figures to illustrate your answer.

2. Explain what is meant by an 'annual percentage change' for consumption and PDI. Use figures to illustrate your answer.

Figure 9.2
It is important to distinguish 'nominal' (or 'money') interest rates from 'real' interest rates. Interest rates fluctuated greatly throughout the 1980s, but the true effect on borrowers and savers can only be assessed by comparing them to the rate of inflation. Interest rates may reach 15 per cent, for example, but if inflation is higher they will be negative in real terms. This means that someone might be able to borrow money and actually pay back less in purchasing power terms than they borrowed.

3. What is the difference between 'real' and 'money' interest rates?

4. Were interest rates higher, lower, or the same at their highest point in 1976 compared to their highest point in 1982? Explain your answer.

Figure 9.3
Financial assets can be classified as short-term or long-term according to their degree of liquidity. Financial assets are essentially pieces of paper which represent a claim on real resources. Some financial assets, such as banknotes, are immediately convertible to real assets without loss and are therefore defined as being very liquid. Liquidity refers to the speed with which an asset can be converted to cash without appreciable loss of value. For example, a rare painting can be quickly converted to cash, but not without the risk of a great loss in value.

5. What proportion of all financial assets in 1984 were short-term assets?

6. Explain why sight deposits at banks are short-term assets whereas equity in life assurance and pension funds are long-term assets.

Figure 9.4
The economic significance of international trends may vary according to the countries involved. The economies of the world are becoming more closely linked as a result of increasing world trade and improving communications. A change in one country's economy will therefore have effects on other economies, and the extent of the effect will depend on that country's share in world trade. It has been said, for example, that 'when America sneezes, the world catches a cold'.

7. Describe the trend in the savings ratio in (a) the United States and (b) Canada between 1984 and 1986.

8. Which trend was likely to have had the greater economic significance internationally, and why?

APPLYING ECONOMIC PRINCIPLES

1. (a) Classical theories of saving, investment and interest tended to suggest that an increase in saving would reduce interest rates, leading to a decrease in the rate of interest and a rise in capital investment. Draw a supply and demand diagram for loanable funds to illustrate this process. (b) John Maynard Keynes, whose major book on economics, *The General Theory of Employment, Interest and Money* was published in 1936, believed that, in an economic depression, an increase in saving could decrease aggregate demand, income, and capital investment. Draw a diagram to illustrate this process. (c) With reference to Figure 9.2, examine the validity of the hypotheses in (a) and (b). (d) How could a rise in investment demand be associated with a rising rate of interest in the market for loanable funds? Draw a diagram to illustrate your answer. What are the possible causes of this?

2. With reference to Figures 9.1 and 9.2: (a) Explain how and why the following may have affected the savings ratio: (i) a rise in real incomes both in the short-term and in the longer term; (ii) a rapid rise in inflation; (iii) a rapid rise in interest rates with unchanged inflation; (iv) a sharp rise in borrowing after 1984. (b) Were households acting rationally by increasing their savings ratio from 1973 to 1975? Explain your answer. (c) How would your answer to (a) (iv) help to explain the apparently inconsistent relationship between real interest rates and savings?

3. (a) Explain what is meant by: (i) personal sector financial assets; (ii) short-term assets, (iii) sight deposits at banks; and (iv) unit trusts. (b) Describe the pattern of personal sector holdings of financial assets shown in Figure 9.3, and explain the reasons for this pattern.

4. Study Figure 9.4 (a) Describe the differences between savings ratios in the countries shown in 1986. (b) What are the possible economic reasons for these differences? (c) What are the possible economic effects of these differences?

FOR FURTHER INVESTIGATION
Conduct a survey amongst young people and adults to find out about savings habits. Try to find out how many people save regularly, why they save, what methods of saving they use, and what percentage of income they save. Find out what factors are likely to change people's savings habits. Write a report on your findings. Use bar charts, tables, etc to present the results of your investigation. Use your summary to compare your findings with the reasons for saving given in this unit and in economics textbooks.

ESSAYS
Refer to the data wherever possible, especially in the first essay.
1. (a) Describe the trends in the UK savings ratio between 1980 and 1986. (b) Describe and explain the link between the savings ratio and interest rates over the same period.
2. What determines the propensity to save? How might it be affected by inflation? [London 6/84]

Spending the taxpayers' money

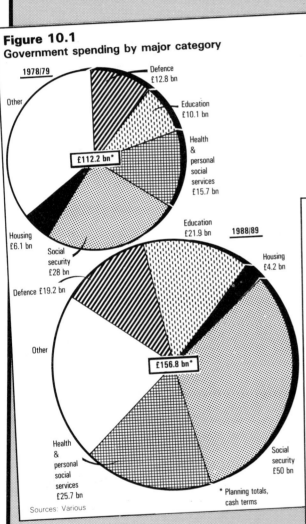

Figure 10.1
Government spending by major category

1978/79

Defence £12.8 bn
Education £10.1 bn
Health & personal social services £15.7 bn
Other
£112.2 bn*
Housing £6.1 bn
Social security £28 bn

1988/89

Education £21.9 bn
Housing £4.2 bn
Social security £50 bn
Defence £19.2 bn
Other
£156.8 bn*
Health & personal social services £25.7 bn

* Planning totals, cash terms

Sources: Various

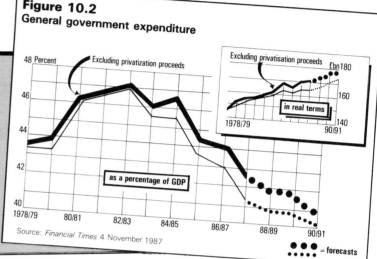

Figure 10.2
General government expenditure

Excluding privatization proceeds
as a percentage of GDP
Excluding privatisation proceeds
in real terms

••••• = forecasts

Source: *Financial Times* 4 November 1987

Figure 10.3
Expenditure on education

Table 1 **Education within the gross domestic product and public expenditure**

	Public spending as % of GDP	Education spending as % of GDP	Education spending as % of public spending
1979/80	43.25	5.3	12.2
1980/81	46	5.7	12.3
1981/82	46.25	5.6	12.0
1982/83	46.75	5.5	11.7
1983/84	45.25	5.4	11.7
1984/85	45.5	5.1	11.3
1985/86	44	4.9	11.1
1986/87	43.25	5.1	11.8
1987/88 plans	42.75	5.0	11.6
1988/89 plans	41.75	4.9	11.7
1989/90 plans	41.25	4.7	11.5

Table 2 **Education current expenditure (England, £m cash)**

	1979/80	1980/81	1981/82	1982/83	1983/84	1984/85	1985/86	1986/87
Central government	1,176	1,476	1,577	1,832	1,941	2,012	2,089	2,176
Local government	7,185	8,722	9,666	10,267	10,836	11,269	11,697	13,007

Table 3 **Real-terms changes (%) in education current expenditure) (England, 1979/80 to 1986/87)**

Local government		Central government
(a) GDP deflator	(b) Local authority volume measure	(GDP deflator)
+8.4	+2.1	+10.8

Table 4 **Education capital expenditure (England, £m cash)**

	1979/80	1980/81	1981/82	1982/83	1983/84	1984/85	1985/86	1986/87
Central government	213	232	237	238	233	247	281	299
Local government	373	472	362	413	424	423	411	471

Figure 10.1
Comparisons between different monetary amounts may not be meaningful where statistics have not been adjusted for inflation. Statistics may be shown sometimes in nominal or absolute terms, i.e. just the bare, unadjusted figures may be given. Sometimes the figures may be adjusted to remove the effects of inflation, and they may be shown 'at constant prices' or in some other appropriate way.

1. By what percentage did government spending increase in cash terms between 1978/79 and 1988/89?

2. What additional information would be needed in order to establish whether government spending increased in real terms over the period?

Figure 10.2
The method used to present statistics may be controversial, even in official government statistics. It is easy to jump to the conclusion that government statistics are in some sense 'neutral'. Although it is true that all statistics are in themselves neutral, the statistics that are selected, or the way in which they are presented or used, may be controversial. For example, the government may measure unemployment by excluding some categories of people that other people would include in the figures.

3. The UK Government in the 1980s was pledged to reducing government spending as a percentage of GDP. Would they have preferred to measure government spending with privatization proceeds included or excluded? Explain your answer.

4. Why might it be considered inappropriate to classify privatization proceeds as negative spending?

Figure 10.3
Increases in value, even in real terms, do not necessarily imply corresponding increases in volume. Inflation distorts statistics in a number of ways, and even figures adjusted for the national inflation rates may fail to adjust for differences in inflation rates in different sectors of the economy. For example, spending on the National Health Service might be shown to be rising significantly in real terms, but if medical equipment prices are moving ahead of changes in the Retail Prices Index, this does not necessarily mean that the quality or quantity of the service has improved.

5. What is meant by the 'GDP deflator'?

6. Give one possible reason to explain the disparity between the change in real local government expenditure on education between 1979/80 and 1986/87, and the much smaller growth in volume.

APPLYING ECONOMIC PRINCIPLES

1. (a) With reference to Figures 10.1 and 10.2 describe the main changes in government expenditure between 1979/80 and 1988/89. (b) Does the growth in expenditure in real terms indicate that an increasing percentage of the nation's resources have been allocated to the government sector? Explain your answer. (c) The UK Government of the 1980s was committed to reducing the share of government expenditure in the economy. Does Figure 10.2 suggest that they were successful or unsuccessful?

2. With reference to Figure 10.3. (a) Define and give examples of: (i) current education expenditure, and (ii) capital education expenditure. (b) What was the percentage increase in (i) current education spending, and (ii) capital education spending between 1979/80 and 1986/87? (c) What possible reasons could account for the difference in the trends? (d) What are the possible economic implications if this trend was reflected in government expenditure as a whole?

3. (a) Define, and give two examples (referring to the data where possible) of (i) public goods, (ii) merit goods, and (iii) natural monopolies. (b) Outline the problems that could arise if the provision of each of these was left to the private sector. (c) Assess the economic costs and benefits of privatizing state schools.

4. Government expenditure is an injection into the circular flow of income and its macroeconomic impact is determined by the size of the multiplier. (a) Define (i) an injection into the circular flow, and (ii) the multiplier. (b) Assume that a closed economy has a national income of £10 billion. Calculate the rise in national income that would follow an increase in government spending of £1 billion where the marginal tax rate is 25 per cent and consumers save 33.33 percent of any rise in disposable income. The rise in spending is financed by borrowing. (c) Illustrate your answer on an appropriate diagram. (d) What difference would be made to your answer to (b) if the rise in expenditure was financed by a rise in taxation rather than a rise in borrowing? (e) What difference would be made to your answer to (b) if the marginal propensity to import in open economy like the UK is taken into account?

5. (a) What is meant by 'expansionary fiscal policy'? (b) What do the data suggest about the Conservative Government's attitude to expansionary fiscal policies? (c) Draw a diagram to illustrate how a rise in government spending could lead to much greater rise in money GDP than real GDP.

FOR FURTHER INVESTIGATION
One of the main debates in the political sphere concerns the role of government expenditure in the economy. Throughout the 1980s the Conservative Government remained pledged to reducing government control over the allocation of resources although, by choice and circumstances, expenditure on some categories of government spending increased. Over a period of a few months collect newspaper articles, preferably from newspapers of different political persuasions, which are concerned with controversy over government spending. Concentrate on the areas of spending shown in Figure 10.1. Write a report which highlights the arguments for and against increased expenditure in the areas concerned.

ESSAYS
Refer to the data wherever possible, especially in the first essay.

1. Describe and account for the government's policy on public expenditure in the 1980s.

2. Discuss the economic arguments for reducing the role of the state in the provision of health, education and housing in the United Kingdom. [AEB 6/85]

Penny pinching

Figure 11.1
Public money 1988–89

Pence in every £1[1]

Receipts	
Income tax	23
National insurance contributions	17
Value added tax	14
Local authority rates	10
Road fuel, alcohol and tobacco duties	10
Corporation tax	9
Capital taxes	3
Interest, dividends	3
North Sea taxation	2
Other	9
Total	**100** (£185bn)

[1] Rounded to the nearest penny

Source: *Economic Progress Report* (Treasury) March 1988

Figure 11.2
Rates of income tax

1978/79		1987/88		1988/89	
Slice of taxable income £	Rate %	Slice of taxable income £	Rate %	Slice of taxable income £	Rate
1 – 750	25	1 – 17 900	27	1–19 300	25
751 – 8000	33	17 901 – 20 400	40	Over 19 300	40
8 001 – 9 000	40	20 401 – 25 400	45		
9 001 – 10 000	45	25 401 – 33 300	50		
10 001 – 11 000	50	33 301 – 41 200	55		
11 001 – 12 500	55	over 41 200	60		
12 501 – 14 000	60				
14 001 – 16 000	65				
16 001 – 18 500	70				
18 501 – 24 000	75				
over 24 000	83				

Sources: AAS. Inland Revenue

Figure 11.3
The public sector borrowing requirement

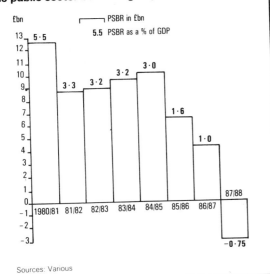

PSBR in £bn

5.5 PSBR as a % of GDP

Sources: Various

Figure 11.4
Total tax revenue as % of GDP

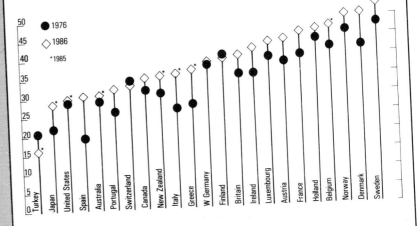

● 1976
◇ 1986
* 1985

Source: OECD and *The Economist* 19 September 1987

Figure 11.1
Government income comes from a variety of sources. It may be commonly imagined that by far the largest source of government income is income tax receipts. In fact income tax in 1988/89 accounted for less than one quarter of government income.

1. Why are National Insurance contributions commonly regarded as a form of taxation?

2. List three sources of government income that might be included under the 'Other' category.

Figure 11.2
Average and marginal tax rates must not be confused. Many people may think that if the basic rate of taxation is announced at 25 per cent this means that most people pay 25 per cent of their income in income tax. This would represent a confusion about the difference between average and marginal tax rates. The marginal tax rate (the basic or standard rate of tax is a marginal rate) refers to the amount of tax someone would pay on an *additional* increment of income, not the percentage of total income paid in income tax.

3. What was the marginal rate of income taxation for someone earning £15 000 in 1988/89?

4. What was the average rate of income taxation in 1988/89 for someone earning £15 000 and receiving the single person's allowance of £2605?

Figure 11.3
A value can be increasing in absolute terms but decreasing in relative terms. Many variables measured in money terms increase from year to year because of inflation. It is therefore useful to analyse the changes in the variables with the effect of inflation removed, or compare them with other variables, to put them in perspective. For example, capital expenditure on education may be rising in absolute terms, but falling relative to education expenditure as a whole.

5. Describe the trends in the PSBR between 1981/82 and 1984/85 in (a) absolute terms, and (b) relative to GDP.

6. To what other variables might the PSBR be compared to assess its economic significance?

Figure 11.4
It cannot be assumed that higher taxation means that taxpayers have less real disposable income. League tables of taxation in different nations are frequently published. They may rank countries according to marginal tax rates, average tax rates, tax as a percentage of GDP, or in some other way. Such rankings can be misleading, however, unless it is remembered that the amount of tax paid by citizens is not a necessary indication of the real value of their income after tax: some high-tax economies enjoy high living standards while some low-tax economies have low living standards.

7. What was tax revenue as a percentage of GDP in 1986 in (a) Turkey, and (b) Sweden?

8. Can it be inferred from the data that the average citizen in Turkey enjoyed a higher living standard than the average citizen in Sweden in 1986? Explain your answer.

APPLYING ECONOMIC PRINCIPLES

1. With reference to Figure 11.1: (a) What is the difference between 'direct' and 'indirect' taxation? (b) Calculate the approximate percentage of total taxation accounted for by direct and indirect taxation in 1988/89. (c) Explain how indirect taxes are regressive in their incidence.

2. Refer to Figure 11.2. (a) What is meant by a 'progressive tax'? (b) (i) Describe the changes in income tax between 1978/79 and 1988/89. (ii) How would these changes have affected the progressive nature of the income tax system?

3. (a) What is meant by 'tax threshold', and how would raising tax thresholds affect taxable income? (b) Why might the government in the 1980s have chosen to reduce taxation by reducing tax rates rather than significantly increasing tax thresholds? (c) What benefits could arise from a policy of significantly increasing tax thresholds rather than reducing tax

4. Refer to Figure 11.3. (a) What is meant by 'the public sector borrowing requirement'? (b) Describe the trends in the PSBR between 1980/81 and 1987/88. (c) Explain how a reduction in the PSBR can be part of (i) a contractionary monetary policy, and (ii) a contractionary fiscal policy. (d) (i) What is meant by 'financial crowding out'? (ii) How will a reduction in the PSBR reduce financial crowding out? (e) For what other reasons might the government have wished to reduce the PSBR during the 1980s? (f) The economy suffered a severe recession in the early 1980s, but by 1987/88 the economy was growing strongly. (i) Explain why it is easier to reduce the PSBR in an economic boom than in a recession; (ii) What criticisms may opponents of the government have made in respect of the PSBR change between 1980/81 and 1981/82 when unemployment was rising rapidly?

5. With reference to Figure 11.4: (a) Describe the trends shown in the line graphs. (b) What factors could account for the trends shown? (c) Why might the Swedish government choose to tax and spend much more relative to its GDP than other rich countries such as the USA? (d) To what extent was the British government successful in reducing tax as a percentage of GDP during the first half of the 1980s?

FOR FURTHER INVESTIGATION
One of the major tax changes in the late 1980s and early 1990s involved the introduction of the community charge and the abolition of local authority rates. Find out about the community charge and how it will be implemented. Find out why the government introduced it, and what criticisms opponents make of it. Write a report about the community charge, assessing it against the four canons of taxation proposed by Adam Smith.

ESSAYS
Refer to the data wherever possible, especially in the first essay.
1. Describe and evaluate the principal changes to income tax made by the government between 1978/79 and 1988/89.
2. Compare and contrast the consequences of a rise in the basic rate of income tax with those following a rise in the rate of value-added tax. [SUJB 6/85]

Left, right, left, right

Figure 12.1

The state and unemployment

THE OUTSTANDING faults of the economic society in which we live are its failure to provide for full employment and its arbitrary and inequitable distribution of wealth and incomes...... The State will have to exercise a guiding influence on the propensity to consume partly through its schemes of taxation, partly by fixing the rate of interest, and partly, perhaps, in other ways. Furthermore, it seems unlikely that the influence of banking policy on the rate of interest will be sufficient by itself to determine an op-timum rate of investment. I conceive, therefore, that a somewhat comprehensive socialisation of investment will prove the only means of securing an approximation to full employment; though this need not exclude all manner of compromises and of devices by which public authority will co-operate with private initiative. But beyond this no obvious case is made out for a system of State Socialism which would embrace most of the economic life of the community. It is not the ownership of the instruments of pro-duction which it is important for the State to assume. If the State is able to determine the aggregate amount of resources devoted to augmenting the instruments and the basic rate of reward to those who own them, it will have accomplished all that is necessary. Moreover, the necessary measures of socialisation can be introduced gradually and without a break in the general traditions of society.

Source: *The General Theory of Employment, Interest and Money* (J. M. Keynes, 1936)

Figure 12.2

Unemployment: a non-Keynesian approach

IS A WORLD recovery truly possible without a large co-ordinated programme of Keynesian stimulus applied internationally?

The evidence is there already. US recovery is in train, as UK recovery has been since early 1981. In the UK it has occurred with tight money and con-tinuously falling public sector deficits. In the US the budget deficit has been rising while there has been confusion about the money supply because of institutional changes in banking practice. Some economists would say that the US government has stimulated the economy in a Keynesian manner by loose money and a rising budget deficit. This is clearly not true. If it were, world (and US) real interest rates would not be at the unprecedentedly high rates they still are. Nor would we have the still present threat of a world debt and banking crisis.

The truth must, on the contrary, be that money *has* been tight and that the high US budget deficit has, within that tight money market, forced developing countries out of the world capital market by penal interest rates. The net contribution to world demand of this process of large deficits has been virtually nil.

To return to the question I posed, the world recovery *is* occurring despite generally tight policies. The non-Keynesian process of recovery is one in which, as producers and workers price their products back into the market, inflation falls, interest rates fall, financial confidence is rebuilt, and spending revives as a result. This non-Keynesian recovery has happened in the UK and the US. And it is significant that it has *not* happened in countries such as France and Eire which tried deliberately to engineer recovery via Keynesian inflationary policies.

In short then, governments must not be tempted from the medicine of tight money by the illusion that loose money will help unemployment. Rather, they must design their taxes, benefits and union laws (in other words, good micro market policies) to further rather than hinder adjustment in the labour market needed to bring down unemployment. If they do, the long-term outlook for unemployment is bright. Even if they do not, the labour market will not break down — but it will take a lot longer to do its job.

Source: *Economic Affairs* July–Sept 1984 (Patrick Minford: "High Employment is Not Permanent")

Figure 12.3

Crowding out

THE MONETARIST view that Government spending, financed by taxes or borrowing from the public, merely displaces or crowds-out private spending is not a new one. It was, in fact, the dominant view before the Keynesian revolution of the 1930s. Both the neo-classical economic establishment and the Government authorities held this view. And even Keynes, strongly aware of these views on fiscal theory, accepted that crowding-out in some form might exist and reduce the effectiveness of the policies he was advocating. The weight of advice on the ineffectiveness of fiscal policy, as an instrument to relieve the depression, strongly influenced the authorities and led to the Treasury attaching great im-portance to the crowding-out argument and pressing the so-called "Treasury View". The established neo-classical view was well expressed by R. G. Hawtrey in his evidence before the Macmillan Committee. Hawtrey denied the usefulness of Government spending, regardless of financing, even under depression conditions. Whether financed out of taxes or loans from savings, Hawtrey believed that increased Government expenditure would merely replace private expenditure. Even if the Government attempted to finance spending out of new bank credit Hawtrey predicted that the result of such a policy would be inflationary, thus forcing up interest rates and leading to a contraction of credit. Such a policy would thus be self defeating since it would mean the end of 'cheap money' for private business. Hawtrey's view summarised the two major contemporary criticisms of proposals for expansionary fiscal policy; either a tax or debt financed policy would merely shift resources from the private sector to the public sector with *no change in the total amount of investment*, or money financed policy would lead to inflation, producing contraction in the private sector via higher interest rates and a deterioration in the balance of payments.

Source: *Economics* Autumn 1984 (P. Robins: "Keynesian Economic Policy & the 'Crowding-Out' Hypothesis")

Figure 12.1
Many influential books are infrequently read and often misunderstood, and they may be subject to different interpretations. The acknowledged great works of economists, especially dead economists, are sometimes misquoted or misunderstood because they are not often read and because their meanings are often obscure. Keynes's *General Theory of Employment, Interest and Money* has had a major influence on the policies of governments since it was published, but probably few politicians have read it. There are the added problems that many parts of the General Theory are subject to different interpretations, and it was written when economic circumstances were substantially different from the present.

1. Some opponents of Keynes have suggested that he was a 'socialist'. Is this view supported by the extract? Explain your answer.

2. Do the conditions in the 1930s, which Keynes described in the first sentence of the extract, apply to modern Britain? Explain your answer.

Figure 12.2
The views of economists and their followers are often arguably misrepresented by opponents. Economists differ greatly in their interpretation of one another's writings, and they may exaggerate or misrepresent the views of economists who hold different views. Opponents of 'Keynesianism' have attributed all kinds of things to Keynes and his followers that Keynes himself may not have supported. It may be necessary, on occasion, to return to original sources to see what economists actually did say.

3. What does Minford allege is the Keynesian view of monetary and interest rate policy?

4. Does the evidence in the extract in Figure 12.1 suggest that Keynes himself necessarily favoured this policy? Explain your answer.

Figure 12.3
Writers on economics often seem to suggest that economists all fit into distinct schools of thought. Economists are often lumped together for the purpose of describing differences in their opinions. Perhaps the two most frequently used divisions are 'monetarists' and 'Keynesians'. In fact economists can rarely be divided so neatly into two categories, and some economists have even suggested that Keynes himself was a monetarist.

5. What evidence is there that Keynes himself accepted certain aspects of classical analysis?

6. Is it possibly only to take **either** a 'Keynesian' **or** a 'monetarist' view of crowding out? Explain your answer.

APPLYING ECONOMIC PRINCIPLES

1. Refer to Figure 12.1. (a) How can the State 'exercise a guiding influence on the propensity to consume through its schemes of taxation'? (b) (i) What does Keynes mean by 'a somewhat comprehensive socialisation of investment'? (ii) What does he mean when he says that he is not advocating a 'system of State Socialism'? (c) How might the State be able to affect 'the aggregate amount of resources devoted to augmenting the instruments (of production)'?

2. With reference to Figure 12.2. (a) Explain what is meant by 'the non-Keynesian process of recovery'? (b) How does this contrast with the Keynesian view of policies to stimulate a recovery? (c) What policies does Minford suggest are necessary to reduce unemployment, and why? (d) Why might unemployment persist, even in the absence of trade unions and unemployment benefits?

3. Refer to Figure 12.3. (a) What is meant by 'crowding out'? (b) In what ways does the article suggest that crowding out can occur? (c) What economic arguments could be made against the crowding out hypothesis?

4. (a) What is meant by the following terms associated particularly with a Keynesian approach to economics: (i) effective demand; (ii) the multiplier effect; (iii) demand management? (b) Use an appropriate diagram to show how an injection of government spending into the economy could lead, via the multiplier, to a disproportionate increase in the level of national income.

5. (a) What is meant by the following terms associated particularly with a monetarist/neo-classical approach to economics: (i) market rigidities; (ii) NAIRU (also known as the natural rate of unemployment), (iii) supply-side economics? (b) Use an appropriate diagram to show how an injection of government spending could lead mainly to an increase in prices as opposed to an increase in output.

FOR FURTHER INVESTIGATION
There are frequent reports in newspapers on unemployment, and articles appear on the subject each month when the unemployment figures are published. Collect some of these articles, looking particularly for comments by government ministers. Highlight passages in the articles which indicate whether the writer, or the person being reported, is broadly in favour of a Keynesian or monetarist approach to the problem of unemployment. Analyse how useful the 'Keynesian/monetarist' division is in analysing the debate about unemployment in the UK.

ESSAYS
Refer to the data wherever possible, especially in the first essay.
1. Describe and explain the essential difference between a 'Keynesian' and a 'monetarist' approach to the problem of unemployment.
2. '...we have gone very far in the past 50 years in expanding the role of government in the economy. That intervention has been costly in economic terms.' (Milton Friedman: *Free to Choose*)
'Strong and effective guidance of the economy by the government will ensure good performance.' (J.K. Galbraith: *Economics and the Art of Controversy*)
Outline the basis for each of these views and, in the light of British experience, say which you feel to be justified. [JMB 6/85]

Signing on

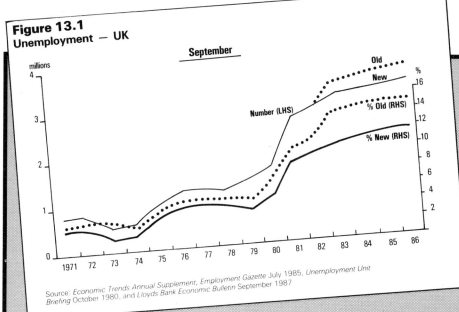

Figure 13.1
Unemployment — UK

September

Source: *Economic Trends Annual Supplement, Employment Gazette* July 1985, *Unemployment Unit Briefing* October 1980, and *Lloyds Bank Economic Bulletin* September 1987

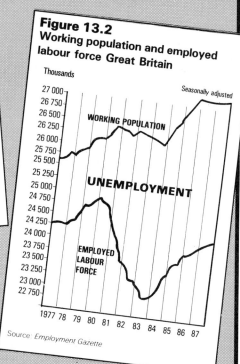

Figure 13.2
Working population and employed labour force Great Britain

Source: *Employment Gazette*

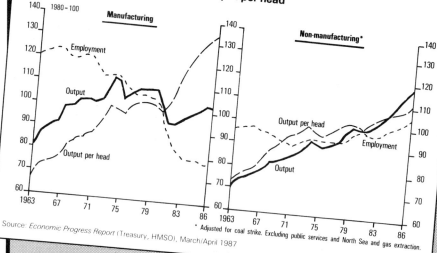

Figure 13.3
Output, employed labour force and output per head

Source: *Economic Progress Report* (Treasury, HMSO), March/April 1987

* Adjusted for coal strike. Excluding public services and North Sea and gas extraction.

Figure 13.4
Youth Training Scheme leavers: by destination

Great Britain		Thousands and percentages		
	YTS members leaving in			
	Apr-Spet 1984	Oct-Mar 1985	Apr-Sept 1985	Oct-Mar 1986
Leavers[2]	**236**	**132**	**281**	**133**
Destination *(percentages)*				
Full-time work				
Same employer	27	17	31	22
Different employer	31	33	24	27
Part-time work	1	1	4	4
Full-time course at				
college/training centre	4	1	4	1
School	–	–	–	–
Different YTS scheme	5	9	5	11
Other	2	2	7	4
Unemployed	30	36	26	32

1 Destination relates to the leavers' activities at the time of the survey.
  Surveys are conducted monthly some 3 months after leaving YTS.
2 Notified to Manpower Services Commission at the end of March 1986.

Source: *Social Trends*, 1988

Figure 13.1
The government may alter the way in which statistics are collected and presented. The method of presenting official statistics is sometimes altered, perhaps reflecting a change in the method of collection. Critics sometimes accuse the government of 'fiddling' the figures for political purposes, whereas the government may claim that an alteration was decided upon by officials rather than politicians. From 1979 the method of calculating unemployment was changed on several occasions. The 'old' lines show unemployment as calculated before these changes; the 'new' lines show unemployment as calculated with the changes included.

1. Did the changes introduced in the method of calculating unemployment increase or decrease the numbers counted as unemployed?
2. Calculate the approximate difference that the 'new' method of calculating unemployment made to the unemployment figures in 1986.

Figure 13.2
The definition of economic terms cannot necessarily be derived from the literal meaning of the words used. The words used by economists often do not mean what they literally appear to mean. For example, the term 'short run' does not mean a given chronological period of time.

3. Explain why the term 'working population' may cause confusion.
4. Explain how employment could fall when the working population is rising.

Figure 13.3
A decline in employment does not necessarily imply a decline in an industry in other respects. The economic condition of industries or group of industries can be analysed in a number of ways. For example, the condition of an industry might be assessed by the percentage change in its turnover in real terms over a number of years; or in terms of the numbers employed in the industry. However, this second measure must be treated with caution because a decline in employment may signify an improvement in the industry in other respects.

5. In what ways might a decline in employment in an industry be accompanied by an improvement in the economic performance of the industry?
6. Can UK manufacturing industry be said to have been in decline from 1982 to 1986? Explain your answer.

Figure 13.4
Statistics are objective but their selection and interpretation are subjective. Statistics, in themselves, are neutral: they offer no opinion nor do they take a particular point of view. However, statistics can be chosen and used to reflect a political or economic opinion. If someone has a particular viewpoint to express they will carefully choose statistics to provide evidence for that viewpoint. People who disagree with this viewpoint may reinterpret the data, or select different data.

7. Explain how the Government could use the data to confirm the success of the YTS, whereas critics of the YTS could use the same figures to expose the shortcomings of the YTS.

APPLYING ECONOMIC PRINCIPLES

1. (a) What is meant by 'trade cycle'? (b) Refer to Figures 13.1 and 13.3. What evidence is there to suggest the importance of the following in causing unemployment: (i) cyclical factors; (ii) structural factors?

2. The working population can increase either as a result of population changes or because people between 16 and 65 who were previously unavailable for work offer themselves for paid employment. With reference to Figure 13.2: (a) Describe and explain the trend in the working population up to 1981. (b) (i) Describe and explain the trend in the working population between 1981 and 1987. (ii) Explain why the sharp rise in employment failed to reduce unemployment significantly in this period.

3. Refer to Figure 13.4 (a) What do the data suggest about the success of the YTS? (b) What other information would you require to assess more accurately whether the benefits of the YTS outweigh the costs? (c) Explain how an increase in training measures is compatible with the following approaches to reducing unemployment: (i) a Keynesian approach; (ii) a supply-side approach.

4. (a) Draw and explain a diagram showing how unemployment can occur as a result of deficient aggregate demand in an economy. (b) According to this model, what policies can the government adopt to reduce unemployment? (c) Explain how the concept of NAIRU is used to criticise Keynesian demand-side approaches to the reduction of unemployment.

5. (a) Explain why the control of inflation is considered by some economists to be of paramount importance to the long-term control of unemployment. (b) (i) Describe some economic policies associated with supply-side economics (ii) Use a diagram to show how supply-side policies can lead to a non-inflationary fall in unemployment. (c) Explain how a Keynesian economist might approach supply-side policies differently from an economist favouring a monetarist neo-classical approach to economic management.

FOR FURTHER INVESTIGATION
One of the problems that has most concerned economists and politicians in recent years is the duration of unemployment — the amount of time people seeking work remain unemployed. Government statistical publications like *Social Trends* contain data on the duration of unemployment. Using appropriate data, write a report which examines the trends in the duration of unemployment. If possible, use figures which analyse the duration in terms of age groups and geographical regions. Examine the factors which have led to the trends, and discuss the consequences and policy implications of the trends.

ESSAYS
Refer to the data wherever possible, especially in the first essay.

1. (a) Describe the trends in unemployment in the UK during the 1970s and 1980s. (b) What (i) population factors, and (ii) other factors could account for these trends?

2. What do you understand by a full employment equilibrium? What determines the level of employment within the UK? [Cambridge 6/86]

The pound in your pocket

Figure 14.1
Index of retail prices (for UK)

Indices for main groups   15 January 1974 = 100

	All items	Food	Alcoholic drink	Tobacco	Housing	Fuel and light	Durable house-hold goods	Clothing and footwear	Transport and vehicles	Miscel-laneous goods	Services	Meals bought and con-sumed outside the home
Annual averages												
1974	108.5	106.1	109.7	115.9	105.8	110.7	107.9	109.4	111.0	111.2	106.8	108.2
1975	134.8	133.3	135.2	147.7	125.5	147.4	131.2	125.7	143.9	138.6	135.5	132.4
1976	157.1	159.9	159.3	171.3	143.2	182.4	144.2	139.4	166.0	161.3	159.5	157.3
1977	182.0	190.3	183.4	209.7	161.8	211.3	166.8	157.4	190.3	188.3	173.3	185.7
1978	197.1	203.8	196.0	226.2	173.4	227.5	182.1	171.0	207.2	206.7	192.0	207.8
1979	223.5	228.3	217.1	247.6	208.9	250.5	201.9	187.2	243.1	236.4	213.9	239.9
1980	263.7	255.9	261.8	290.1	269.5	313.2	226.3	205.4	288.7	276.9	262.7	290.0
1981	295.0	277.5	306.1	358.2	318.2	380.0	237.2	208.3	322.6	300.7	300.8	318.0
1982	320.4	299.3	341.4	413.3	358.3	433.3	243.8	210.5	343.5	325.8	331.6	341.7
1983	335.1	308.8	366.5	440.9	367.1	465.4	250.4	214.8	366.3	345.6	342.9	364.0
1984	351.8	326.1	387.7	489.0	400.7	478.8	256.7	214.6	374.7	364.7	357.3	390.8
1985	373.2	336.3	412.1	532.5	452.3	499.3	263.9	222.9	392.5	392.2	381.3	413.3
1986	385.9	347.3	430.6	584.9	478.1	506.0	266.7	229.2	390.1	409.2	400.5	439.5

Source: *Annual abstract of statistics*

Figure 14.2
Return on US investments

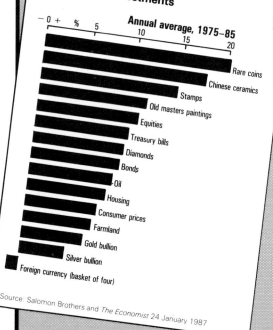

Annual average, 1975–85

Rare coins
Chinese ceramics
Stamps
Old masters paintings
Equities
Treasury bills
Diamonds
Bonds
Oil
Housing
Consumer prices
Farmland
Gold bullion
Silver bullion
Foreign currency (basket of four)

Source: Salomon Brothers and *The Economist* 24 January 1987

Figure 14.3
Inflation in the UK, and its possible determinants

Year	1 % change in retail prices	2 & change in average weekly earnings	3 % change in import prices	4 % change in money stock (£M3)	5 Unemploy-ment (%)	6 Unfilled vacancies (%)
1970	6	12	4	9	2.6	0.8
1971	9	11	5	14	3.1	0.6
1972	7	13	5	27	3.5	0.6
1973	9	14	28	27	2.4	1.4
1974	16	18	46	11	2.4	1.3
1975	24	27	14	6	3.7	0.6
1976	17	16	22	10	5.0	0.6
1977	16	9	16	9	5.3	0.7
1978	8	13	4	16	5.2	0.9
1979	13	15	7	13	4.8	1.0
1980	18	21	10	19	6.1	0.6
1981	12	13	8	14	9.5	0.4
1982	9	9	8	9	11.0	0.5
1983	5	8	9	11	12.1	0.6
1984	5	6	9	10	12.6	0.7
1985	6	9	4	12	13.1	0.7

Source: M. Artis (ed.), The U.K. Economy: A Manual of Applied Economics (Prest and Coppock), George Weidenfeld & Nicolson Ltd.

Figure 14.1

Index numbers allow immediate comparison of percentage changes from a base date, not from other dates. Index numbers show the percentage change in a figure from the base date. For example, it can be easily seen that retail prices in general rose by 285.9 per cent from 1974 to 1986 — i.e. prices nearly trebled. However, some calculation is needed to work out percentage changes between one date and another, when neither is the base date.

1. What was the percentage change in transport and vehicle prices between 1974 and 1986?

2. (**a**) What was the percentage change in transport and vehicle prices between 1985 and 1986? (**b**) What was unusual about this percentage change?

Figure 14.2

Returns on assets can be in the form of interest, profits and dividends, or in terms of an increase in the value of the asset. When people invest they hope to make a financial gain: the gain could be in the form of a regular income, or it could arise as a result of an appreciation in the value of the asset. For example, a stock in a company will yield annual interest and it may also rise in value on the Stock Exchange.

3. Can it be inferred from the data that stamps were a better investment than equities in the US between 1975 and 1985? Explain your answer.

Figure 14.3

It may be possible to make inferences about the general state of the economy from a variety of data. The economy tends to move in a cycle of economic activity (the 'trade cycle'). The position of the economy on the trade cycle may be discovered by examining data on, for example, consumption, investment and interest rates, and from the kind of data shown in this table.

4. Can it be inferred from the data that the economy was on an upswing on the trade cycle (**a**) between 1972 and 1973, and (**b**) between 1980 and 1981? Explain your answer.

ANALYSING ECONOMIC PRINCIPLES

1. Refer to Figure 14.1. (**a**) How is inflation measured using the Index of Retail Prices? (**b**) What problems are involved in measuring inflation using the Retail Price Index?

2. With reference to Figure 14.1: (**a**) Describe and explain the difference in the price changes of durable household goods and housing between 1974 and 1986. (**b**) Explain how government policy could have helped to account for the different rate of increase in prices of alcoholic drink and tobacco. (**c**) Why might changes in income elasticity of demand create problems for economists constructing the Retail Price Index?

3. (**a**) What are the main effects of inflation? (**b**) In what ways does Figure 14.2 suggest that individuals on higher incomes might be better able to hedge against inflation than those on low incomes? (**c**) Do the data suggest a trade-off between liquidity and profitability? Explain your answer.

4. (**a**) How is inflation generally related to the trade cycle in theory? (**b**) Refer to Figure 14.3. Does the relationship in (**a**) hold for the period between 1970 and 1985? Give evidence to explain your answer. (**c**) How are exogenous shocks to the UK economy in this period relevant in explaining high inflation in periods of recession?

5. (**a**) What is the 'Phillips Curve'? (**b**) Why was the Phillips Curve considered to be a guide to policy makers in the 1960s? With reference to Figure 14.3: (**c**) Explain why the Phillips Curve was discredited in the 1970s. (**d**) How did the Expectations-Augmented Phillips Curve attempt to explain the breakdown of the conventional Phillips Curve relationship in the 1970s? Illustrate your answer with a diagram. (**e**) What alternative explanations might there be for the 'stagflation' of the 1970s? (**f**) Did the Phillips Curve relationship return in the 1980s? Support your answer with evidence.

FOR FURTHER INVESTIGATION

Hyperinflation refers to a situation where inflation increases very rapidly and money becomes almost worthless. The most famous case of hyperinflation occurred in Germany in the 1920s, but more recently countries in South America have experienced hyperinflation. Write an account of a country's experience of hyperinflation. Find out how hyperinflation affected the process of exchange, and what consequences it had for the economy concerned.

ESSAYS

Refer to the data wherever possible, especially in the first essay.

1. (**a**) Describe the UK experience of inflation in the 1970s and 1980s. (**b**) What evidence is there that inflation in this period was (**i**) demand-pull; (**ii**) cost-push?

2. Compare the relative costs of unemployment and inflation on an economy. Can policy makers choose the level of unemployment and inflation for an economy? [JMB 6/85]

15 Shipbuilding

A sunset industry

Figure 15.1
Profile of British shipbuilding — 1984/85

Date nationalized	1977
Employment	41 000 (down 53% since nationalization)
Total assets	£0.7 bn
Turnover	£0.87 bn
Loss (current cost)	£173 bn

Source: *The Economist* 12 October 1985

Figure 15.2
Too much by half

World shipbuilding capacity (m gross tonnes)

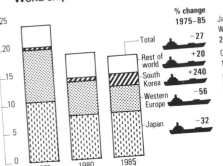

	% change 1975–85
Total	−27
Rest of world	+20
South Korea	+240
Western Europe	−56
Japan	−32

Ships completed in 1985 (by country)

Total: 14.2m gross tonnes

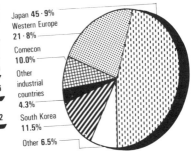

Japan 45·9%
Western Europe 21·8%
Comecon 10.0%
Other industrial countries 4.3%
South Korea 11.5%
Other 6.5%

Source: *The Economist*, 7 June 1987

Figure 15.3
What happens when this work runs out?

BS yard	Current orders	Completion date
Govan	1 passenger RO/RO ferry	March 1987
Austin & Pickersgill	1 multi purpose cargo vessel	First half 1987
	1 barge	First half 1987
	12 ferries	June 1987 to mid-1989
Sunderland	1 diving support vessel	First half 1987
	1 diving support vessel	First half 1987
	1 crane ship	June 1987 to mid-1989
	13 ferries	April 1987
Appledore	1 dredger 5K	September 1987
	1 dredger 2K	February 1988
Ferguson (Port Glasgow)	1 passenger RO/RO ferry	Early 1987
Ferguson (Troon)	1 research vessel	Early 1987
Smith's dock	1 SD King cargo vessel	July 1987
Clark Kincaid (Greenock)	1 engine	

Source: *Guardian* 16 December 1986

Figure 15.4

Subsidising shipbuilding

A MAKE-or-break meeting of European industry ministers in Brussels next Monday will decide whether the EEC wants to continue competing in world shipbuilding markets.

The meeting has been called to vote on whether to increase the subsidies which can be given by EEC governments to shipyards. At one extreme, Britain is arguing that its shipbuilding industry will be wiped out without a huge increase in subsidies. And although there is some sympathy for the British viewpoint from West Germany, Denmark and Holland, other member states will argue strongly in favour of abolishing all subsidy levels in line with the long term policy goals of the Community.

The December 22 meeting is vital, because the existing EEC Fifth Directive which governs shipbuilding aid expires at the end of the year. British officials insist that without an increase in the present shipbuilding intervention subsidy from 26 per cent to a comparable 36 per cent, British and other European yards will be wiped out by fierce Far Eastern competition by the end of the decade. if subsidies are increased Britain maintains that the industry may yet survive to cash-in on an anticipated increase in world shipbuilding orders in the early 1990s.

Cynics might argue that it is too late to talk about saving the British, or European shipbuilding industries. The drastic rundown of the British industry was highlighted by industry minister, Giles Shaw, earlier this month when he answered questions raised in the House of Commons by Gordon Brown, Labour MP for Dunfermline East, Mr Shaw's statistical snapshot showed that during the first half of this year British yards have won 1.6 per cent of all new shipbuilding orders against 2.7 per cent in 1985 and 50 per cent of all shipbuilding orders thirty years before that when the industry was at its peak.

Source: *Guardian* 16 December 1986

Figure 15.1

The same concept can have different names in different contexts. Economists do not necessarily use the same names as people in business to describe what may be essentially the same concept. For example, someone may refer to their 'overheads' whereas an economist might use the term 'fixed costs' to describe the same concept. Another example is average cost which is often called cost per unit.

1. Which item in the data is the same as total revenue?
2. Which item would include fixed and working capital?

Figure 15.2

A distinction may need to be made between capacity, and the amount actually produced. The amount that a firm, industry or economy actually produces need not be the same as the amount they could produce at full capacity, i.e. if they were producing the maximum possible. The term 'capacity utilization rate' can be used to describe the ratio of actual output to full capacity output. It should be noted that 'capacity' can also refer in some contexts to output at minimum average cost.

3. What was the capacity utilization rate for shipbuilding in 1985 in (a) Japan, and (b) the world?
4. Did the shipbuilding industry necessarily have more unused capacity in 1985 than in 1975? Explain your answer.

Figure 15.3

The importance of time lags in economics must be recognised. A study of economic theory, particularly supply and demand analysis, often leaves the impression that economic change is instantaneous. In reality, however, the implication of economic decisions take a considerable time to make their full impact. For example, the performance of a company that is involved in long-term projects in any one year will be affected by its investment decisions in previous years.

5. Which shipyard appeared to have the most secure long-term future in December 1986? Explain your answer.

Figure 15.4

Economic arguments are likely to be affected by political interests. It may be easy to jump to the conclusion when reading articles that all arguments put forward by economists and politicians in favour of a particular policy are justifiable primarily from an economic standpoint. There may be good (or not so good!) political or social reasons for the arguments, even if the supporters of the arguments are not aware of them or do not choose to acknowledge them. For example, a decision to privatize a nationalized industry could be taken, according to critics, in order to raise revenue and gain political advantage from being able to cut taxes before an election; the decision might be justified publicly, however, on the grounds of increasing competition and efficiency.

6. In what ways may the British Government have been putting the interests of Britain before those of the EC when arguing for an increase in subsidies for shipbuilding?

APPLYING ECONOMIC PRINCIPLES

1. (a) What is meant by 'nationalization'? (b) (i) What arguments might be given in favour of nationalizing industries? (ii) Which arguments may have applied to shipbuilding in 1977? Illustrate your answer with reference to Figure 15.3 and 15.4. (c) Refer to Figure 15.1. To what extent do the figures suggest that nationalization of the shipbuilding industry failed? (d) What other information would you need to help determine whether nationalization was a failure? (e) Refer to Figures 15.1 and 15.3. Why would it have been difficult for the government to have privatized British Shipbuilders in 1984/85?

2. (a) What is meant by 'overcapacity'? Use information from Figure 15.2 to illustrate your answer. (b) What does overcapacity imply about (i) the scale of production in the industry, and (ii) average fixed costs? (c) Draw a cost curve diagram and illustrate overcapacity in an industry. (d) Refer to Figure 15.2. What was the capacity of Europe in (i) 1975 and (ii) 1985? (iii) What percentage decrease did that represent? (e)

(i) Which country experienced the greatest increase in capacity between 1975 and 1985? Support your answer with figures. (ii) What factors might have accounted for the growth in capacity in this country compared to the traditional producers like the UK?

3. Shipbuilding is a localized industry. (a) What is meant by a 'localized' industry? (b) With reference to Figure 15.3, name three traditional shipbuilding areas in Britain. (c) What external costs are associated with the decline in shipbuilding?

4. Refer to Figure 15.4. (a) What was the view on subsidies for shipbuilding presented by (i) most EC members, and (ii) the UK? (b) What arguments were put forward by the UK officials to support their view? (c) What arguments could have been put forward by opponents of the British view? (d) Draw a supply and demand diagram showing the effect in the short-term and in the longer-term of a withdrawal of subsidies, according to UK officials.

FOR FURTHER INVESTIGATION
Write an account of the shipbuilding industry in the UK. Do not rely solely on the information in this unit, but visit a local library to obtain further information. Many sources of information will quote further sources that you can consult. Where possible, apply economic principles to your analysis, and support the account with appropriate statistics presented in a variety of forms, such as tables, graphs and charts. Conclude with a prediction about the future of the shipbuilding industry in the UK.

ESSAYS
Refer to the data wherever possible, especially in the first essay.
1. (a) Describe the condition of the shipbuilding industry in the mid-1980s. (b) (i) Where are most ships built in the world at present? (ii) Why has the centre of shipbuilding moved away from Europe?
2. Should the shipbuilding industry in the UK be allowed to die?

A sunrise industry

Figure 16.1
The UK manufacturing industry as a whole and the electronics industry compared.

Value of production (£ million)	1979	1986
Manufacturing industry	£155 365	£216 574 (est)

Value of sales (£ million)		
Office machinery & data processing equipment	£ 1 107	£ 3 400
Electrical & electronic engineering	£ 9 713	£ 17 169

Source: *Annual Abstract of Statistics*

Figure 16.2
The UK electronics industry and overseas trade

	1975		1980		1986	
	Imports	Exports	Imports	Exports	Imports	Exports
Office machines, data processing machinery (£ million)	543	515	1 393	1 346	4 545	3 562
Telecommunications, sound recording/reproducing equipment (£ million)	333	428	824	713	2 402	1 402
Electrical machinery, apparatus & appliances (£ million)	578	821	1 518	1 799	4 446	3 383

Source: *Annual Abstract of Statistics*

Figure 16.3
Employment in the UK electronics industry

(000) June each year

	1982	1983	1984	1985	1986
All manufacturing	5 863	5 225	5 409	5 365	5 239
All services	13 446	13 501	13 836	14 192	14 495
All industries & services	21 414	21 067	21 238	21 509	21 594
Office machinery, data processing equipment	79	81	84	91	91
Electrical & electronic engineering	633	612	607	594	569
— Wires, cables, batteries* & other electrical equipment	245	228	220	217	204
— Telecommunication equipment*	190	185	180	175	167
— Other electronic & electrical* equipment	191	191	200	195	191

(* figures for GB)

Source: *Annual Abstracts*

Figure 16.4

The UK information technology industry

THE UK'S prospects in information technology are not, on the face of things, particularly promising. Its share of the world market in data processing, telecommunications and computing services remains stubbornly small at only just over 5 per cent. Last year, Britain exported £6.8bn of information technology equipment and imported £8.9bn, a shortfall of £2.1bn.

It boasts one mainframe computer manufacturer, International Computers, with world-wide sales of rather less than 4 per cent of those of the industry leader, International Business Machines.

Nevertheless, measured by value of installed equipment, ICL part of the STC group, is the only UK-owned company to figure in the UK "top ten" hardware suppliers.

It takes second place to IBM; all the rest are US-owned with the exception of Nixdorf in ninth place.

Britain's programme of research into advanced computing technology, the Alvey initiative, has come to the end of its term and, despite good evidence of solid progress in many areas, the Government is reluctant to commit further funding on the scale demanded.

Source: *Financial Times* 4 January 1988

Figure 16.1
Figures showing the increase or decrease in a variable may be presented in a number of different ways. Statistics used to show the growth or decline in some variable may be presented in a number of different ways. Sometimes just nominal figures are given, and on other occasions the nominal figures may have been translated into index numbers or percentages. All the methods of presentation have advantages and disadvantages, and all should therefore be treated with caution.

1. Present the information shown as index numbers, with 1979 as a base.
2. What advantages and disadvantages for economic analysis would the index number presentation have over the unmodified figures?

Figure 16.2
The units used for the measurement of values must be correctly recognized. It is very easy to make a mistake about the units in which something is being measured. For example, a table of population figures may have in small print at the top '(000s)'. A figure of 56 000 in the table should then be interpreted as 56 000 000 and not 56 000.

3. What was the value of imports of office machinery etc in 1975?
4. How would this value be expressed in £ billion?

Figure 16.3
The size of industries can be measured in several ways. There are many ways of measuring the size of industries. For example, an industry could be measured in terms of the capital employed in the industry and it could also be measured in terms of the value of output produced. Employment is a frequently used way of measuring size, but increasingly it could be the most misleading in assessing the importance of an industry to the economy.

5. What was the percentage fall in employment in the telecommunication equipment industry between 1982 and 1986?
6. Can it be inferred from the data that the telecommunication equipment industry became economically less significant between 1982 and 1986? Explain your answer.

Figure 16.4
Industries may be classified into categories and sub-categories. The Department of Trade and Industry places industries in different classes for the purpose of analysis. These classes are divided and further sub-divided. For example, one category of goods is classed as 'Metal goods, engineering and vehicle industries': this category can be divided further into other categories, for example, 'Electrical and electronic engineering'. There are further divisions within this sub-category, such as 'Domestic-type electric appliances'. Newspapers sometimes make up their own unofficial categories, which may reflect the rapidly changing nature of industry.

7. Which parts of the electrical and electronic engineering industry are classified in the article as 'information technology'?

APPLYING ECONOMIC PRINCIPLES

1. (a) Use Figures 16.1 and 16.3 to calculate the percentage change in (i) the value of sales of the electrical and electronics industry between 1979 and 1986, and (ii) employment between 1982 and 1986. (b) What does your answer to (a) suggest about the balance of factors of production in the electrical and electronics industry? (c) If the trends shown by your answer to (a) continue, what is likely to happen to (i) variable costs, and (ii) fixed costs in this industry in the future? Explain your answer.

2. (a) Refer to Figure 16.2. Calculate the percentage growth between 1975 and 1986 in the value of (i) import sales (ii) export sales of the electronics industry as a whole. (b) Refer to Figure 16.4. Did the position appear to be improving from the UK point of view in 1987? Explain your answer. (c) In which of the three categories shown in Figure 16.2 has the UK fared least badly in terms of foreign trade? (d) What factors might account for the relatively poor UK trade performance in high technology products?

3. Refer to Figure 16.3 (a) (i) Describe the trends in employment in electrical and electronic engineering compared to employment in manufacturing and services between 1982 and 1986. (ii) What reasons could account for the difference in these trends? (b) Explain why manufacturing industry will provide few new jobs in the future.

4. The costs of producing computers has fallen rapidly. The cost of producing a 64K random-access memory chip, for example, fell from about $200 in 1979 to below $3 by 1985: (a) What are the factors that could have accounted for the fall in the average price of a microchip? (b) Use a supply and demand diagram to explain why the price of computers has fallen rapidly in recent years. (c) What are the main factors accounting for the large growth in the sales of the office machinery and data-processing equipment industry shown in Figure 16.1?

5. Refer to Figure 16.4. (a) What evidence is there to show (i) that information technology is dominated by large firms (ii) that the UK information technology industry is dominated by foreign firms? (b) What reasons could account for the domination of large firms in the industry? (c) Should the government encourage or discourage foreign firms that wish to set up information technology productive capacity in the UK? Give reasons for your answer.

FOR FURTHER INVESTIGATION
The electronics industry is geographically concentrated in the UK. Try to find out where the industry is located, and the factors that account for its location. Draw a map indicating the main areas of concentration and, if possible, the location of some of the largest firms. Write a report on the location of the electronics industry in the UK based on your findings.

ESSAYS
Refer to the data wherever possible, especially in the first essay.
1. 'The electronics industry is of little benefit to the UK: it helps neither employment nor our foreign trade position.' Discuss.
2. If the government were to announce that it intended to promote the development of a number of British industries, what criteria should underlie the selection of those industries? [Oxford 6/86]

Company profile

Figure 17.1

Birmid Qualcast

Birmid Qualcast is a leading manufacturer of such household branded products as Potterton boilers, Qualcast, Atco and Webb lawnmowers and New World gas cookers. The Group also manufactures a range of ceramic and plastic products for bathrooms. These businesses comprise the consumer products activities.

The Group also has important industrial products available. These comprise, in the main, castings businesses which are leading producers of a wide variety of components for use in automotive, aerospace and defence industries and numerous other applications. The Group's businesses are predominantly located in the UK and currently employ approximately 6 800 people.

Turnover and operating results

| | 1987 | | 1986 | |
Analysis	Turnover £000	Operating profit £000	Turnover £000	Operating profit (loss) £000
Consumer Products Group	134 118	18 069	108 112	12 732
Industrial Products Group	83 319	4 554	95 675	2 174
Other net income (costs)	—	1 529		(564)
	217 437	24 152	203 787	14 342

Other net income includes pension contribution holiday of £2,377,000 (1986: Nil).

Geographical analysis of turnover

United Kingdom	190 113	175 656
Africa	2 341	3 053
America	5 738	7 261
Asia	519	906
Australasia	92	137
Europe—EEC countries	13 597	11 922
Europe—other countries	5 037	4 852
	217 437	203 787

Employee information

The average number of persons employed by the Group during the period is analysed below:

	1987	1986
Consumer Products Group	4 163	2 655
Industrial Products Group	2 773	3 826
Company	22	25
	6 958	6 506

Group employment costs:	£000	£000
Aggregate gross wages and salaries	56 488	58 233
Social security costs	4 152	4 398
Other pension costs	1 190	3 901
	61 830	66 532

Source: Birmid Qualcast *Report & Accounts* 1987

Figure 17.2
Ownership of shares
At 31st October, 1987

Size of shareholdings

	Number of separate holdings	%
1 – 500	2 584	32
501 – 1 000	1 807	22
1 001 – 2 500	2 082	26
2 501 – 5 000	852	10
5,001 – 10,000	392	5
Over 10,000	440	5
	8 157	100

Category of shareholder

	Number of shares held (millions)	%
Banks and nominees	38.2	53
Insurance companies	8.1	11
Investment and trust companies	10.1	14
Pension and welfare funds	2.0	3
Others	13.9	19
	72.3	100

Source: Birmid Qualcast *Report & Accounts* 1987

Figure 17.3

FIVE YEAR RECORD

	1987 £m	1986 £m	1985 £m	1984 £m	1983 £m
Profit and loss account					
Turnover	217.4	203.8	202.7	207.4	175.8
Operating profit	24.1	14.4	12.2	12.6	10.1
Interest payable less receivable	(1.5)	(1.3)	(2.1)	(1.3)	(1.5)
Profit before taxation	22.6	13.1	10.1	11.3	8.6
Taxation	(6.5)	(2.8)	(2.1)	(2.1)	(0.8)
Profit after taxation	16.1	10.3	8.0	9.2	7.8
Balance sheet					
Tangible fixed assets	38.7	34.6	34.0	31.7	30.3
Investments	0.9	—	—	—	—
Net current assets	43.2	40.1	35.3	29.6	33.5
	82.8	74.7	69.3	61.3	63.8
Creditors: amounts falling due after more than one year	(17.5)	(16.6)	(13.4)	(6.5)	(10.8)
Provisions for liabilities and charges	(0.5)	—	—	—	—
Net assets	64.8	58.1	55.9	54.8	53.0
Issued share capital	18.1	16.5	16.5	16.5	16.5
Reserves	46.7	41.6	39.4	38.3	36.5
	64.8	58.1	55.9	54.8	53.0
Earnings per share	23.6p	15.6p	12.1p	13.9p	11.8p
Dividends per share	7.75p	4.75p	3.75p	3.25p	2.33p

Source: Birmid Qualcast *Report & Accounts* 1987

DATA ANALYSIS SKILLS **17**

Figure 17.1
Data may need to be represented in different forms to give greater prominence to trends. Statistical information can be presented in many different ways. The figures may be unadjusted, or modified in the form of, for example, index numbers or percentages. Different methods of presentation have different strengths and weaknesses.

1. Imagine that the Board of Directors of Birmid Qualcast were particularly interested in the change from 1985 to 1987 in the percentage of sales that were accounted for by markets outside the UK. Represent the relevant information in an appropriate form to emphasize the change.

2. Suggest an appropriate method for showing the proportion of Birmid Qualcast's employees found in different product groups of the company in 1987.

Figure 17.2
Care must be taken with the interpretation of apparently straightforward information. Companies present information about share ownership in different ways. One method is to show how many shareholdings there are of different sizes. Another method is to analyse the type of shareholder and show how many shares each type owns. It may not be easy,

however, to interpret and manipulate apparently straightforward information.

3. What was the average number of shares per shareholding?

4. Do the data suggest that 5 per cent of shares were held by shareholders with over 10 000 shares? Explain your answer.

Figure 17.3
Figures may need to be calculated from other figures in order to assess economic performance. Companies do not necessarily present their financial information in a form that includes adjustment for inflation. This would make it difficult to assess the performance of the company in real terms. However, it might be possible to work out a measure of performance by, for example, relating one set of figures to another.

5. What additional information would you need to assess whether the company's turnover increased in real terms between 1985 and 1986?

6. Calculate the ratio of operating profit to turnover for the years from 1983 to 1987. What does this suggest about the company's performance?

APPLYING ECONOMIC PRINCIPLES

1. Refer to Figure 17.1. (a) Which products group had the highest productivity in 1987? (b) Which products group had the highest profit per employee in 1987? (c) Are either or both of the above measures good measures of efficiency? Explain your answer.

2. (a) Study Figure 17.1. What evidence is there that Birmid Qualcast has grown partly through integration? (b) For what reasons might this have occurred? (c) In what circumstances might internal growth be preferable to external growth for Birmid Qualcast?

3. (a) Refer to Figure 17.2 and describe the pattern of share ownership of Birmid Qualcast. (b) Would you expect the pattern of share ownership for Birmid Qualcast to be typical for British industry as a whole? Explain your answer. (c) (i) How might the pattern of share ownership affect the influence of individual shareholders over the firm? (ii) How might this affect the aims of the firm?

4. (a) What is meant by 'profit'? (b) What factors affect the level of a company's profits? (c) Refer to Figures 17.2 and 17.3. What was the total dividend payment to insurance companies in 1987? (d) In what other ways can a firm allocate its profits?

(e) What are the advantages and disadvantages of a company distributing a relatively high percentage of profits in a given year to its shareholders?

5. Sketch supply and demand diagrams to show how the price and output of specific Birmid Qualcast products could be affected by the following market changes. (a) A rival firm produces a very cheap and efficient new hover mower. (b) There is a steep rise in the price of iron used for casting. (c) Birmid Qualcast launches a very successful advertising campaign for its mowers. (d) Wages in the heating division rise more than productivity.

6. Companies like Birmid Qualcast are affected by changes outside their control in the national and international economies. How might the company have been affected by the following events in recent years? (a) A very large increase in both interest rates and the exchange rate of the pound in 1979. (b) The boom in house prices and house building in the South East in the mid- to late 1980s. (c) Wet summers in the mid-1980s (the company is a major supplier of irrigation equipment).

FOR FURTHER INVESTIGATION
The annual reports of companies are generally freely available. Find out the name of another mainly British-based engineering company and obtain a copy of its report. Write an analysis of the company under the following headings: (a) product range (b) contribution of individual divisions to turnover and profitability. (c) employment characteristics (d) pattern of ownership, (e) performance in recent years. Compare the performance of the company with that of Birmid Qualcast over years for which you have comparative information.

ESSAYS
Refer to the data wherever possible, especially in the first essay.

1. (a) Would Birmid Qualcast have been satisfied with its economic performance between 1983 and 1987? Explain your answer. (b) What other information would have enabled you to give a better answer to this question?

2. What long-term difficulties are posed for UK companies like Birmid Qualcast by (a) the development of newly industrialized countries like Singapore; (b) microtechnology?

Small is beautiful

Figure 18.1
Size of manufacturing units, 1987

Number of units	Total	Analysis by number of employees							
		1–9	10–19	20–49	50–99	100–199	200–499	500–999	1 000 and over
All manufacturing industries	154 474	103 588	18 268	15 902	7 298	4 759	3 217	963	479
Extraction and preparation of metalliferous ores and metal manufacturing	1 684	684	214	312	202	122	99	27	24
Extraction of minerals not elsewhere specified and manufacture of non-metallic mineral products	7 254	4 626	1 051	790	358	210	157	50	12
Chemical industry and production of man-made fibres	4 142	2 192	547	496	353	237	180	93	44
Manufacture of metal goods not elsewhere specified	14 461	9 310	2 033	1 752	737	374	196	53	6
Mechanical engineering	25 286	17 265	3 119	2 790	987	561	378	125	61
Manufacture of office machinery and data processing equipment	1 189	846	129	83	49	36	23	15	8
Electrical and electronic engineering	10 617	6 840	1 117	1 063	562	428	365	147	95
Manufacture of motor vehicles and parts thereof	2 429	1 205	363	351	187	123	107	50	43
Manufacture of other transport equipment	2 474	1 546	259	264	148	96	66	27	68
Instrument engineering	2 812	1 650	408	381	177	109	70	15	2
Food, drink and tobacco manufacturing industries	11 129	6 556	1 526	1 209	641	585	462	150	—
Textile industry	5 310	2 989	676	441	294	40	—	—	—
Manufacture of leather and leather goods	1 443	1 000	183	158	60	31	11	—	—
Footwear and clothing industries	12 515	8 369	1 447	1 235	619	470	240	97	38
Timber and wooden furniture industries	14 137	10 633	1 406	1 321	451	215	62	37	12
Manufacturing of paper and paper products; printing and publishing	23 223	17 272	2 476	1 900	691	479	299	76	30
Processing of rubber and plastics	5 482	3 055	747	764	422	282	172	30	10
Other manufacturing industries	8 837	7 550	658	392	159	78	—	—	—

Source: *Annual Abstract of Statistics*

Figure 18.2
Distribution of firms by turnover, 1985 (UK)

	Turnover size (% of total firms)			% of total business	% of total employment
	Up to £¼m	£¼–1m	£1m+		
Agriculture, forestry and fishing	91.1	8.0	0.9	9.5	1.6
Mining and quarrying and public utilities	55.5	23.3	21.2	0.1	2.9
Manufacturing	69.1	18.7	12.2	10.7	25.8
Construction	86.5	10.3	3.2	14.3	4.5
Services	83.4	11.4	5.2	65.4	65.2
All businesses	83.0	11.7	5.3	100.0	100.0

Source: *Midland Bank Review* Spring 1987, *Annual Abstract of Statistics* 1987 and *British Economy Survey* Autumn 1987

Figure 18.3

Small firms and their advantages

It is impossible to find a single accurate definition of a small firm. The most widely-used statistical definitions are in terms of employment or turnover, though the labour intensity of the business concerned will obviously affect the reliability of employment as an indicator of size. However, care must be taken in interpreting the data, as cut-off points vary. Small firms have been defined as employing fewer than 20, 100, and 200 people, and many other figures in between these. Similar caution must be applied to data using turnover.

The concern of policy makers is the possible advantages of encouraging small businesses. Economists define an increase in production efficiency as a reduction in average costs of production. Small firms may be able to operate more efficiently than large firms if the market is highly specialised or localised; where the production process is not suited to mass production methods and the high fixed costs of large firms enable small firms to be competitive; where large firms are experiencing diseconomies of scale; and in particular where small firms can respond more flexibly to changes in market conditions. Small firms may pro-

vide a macroeconomic advantage in the reduction of unemployment if they create employment through their greater labour intensity, and in particular offset a decline in employment in larger industries. Any examination of small firms in the British economy provides some evidence of the validity of the suggested economic advantages of small firms in terms of efficiency and employment gains, although clearly it is often difficult to identify and measure these accurately.

Source: *British Economy Survey* Autumn 1987

Figure 18.1
It is important to identify the different terms used to describe industries and parts of industries. Newspapers, business managers and economists use various terms to describe industry and its component parts. The definitions used by economists usually have precise meanings which should not be confused.

1. Which **one** of the following means the same as 'establishment': (**a**) enterprise, (**b**) firm, (**c**) industry, (**d**) production unit?

2. Which two of the remaining three words in the list have the same meaning as each other?

Figure 18.2
Where data have been selected from a variety of sources, they may have been selected to support hypotheses. The government and other organizations publish a mass of statistics each year. Economists will often select data in order to make a particular point or support a particular hypothesis. It is important to look at a table of statistics as a whole to try and find out why a particular sample of statistics has been selected.

3. Formulate a hypothesis that could be supported by the statistics.

Figure 18.3
It may be difficult to define some very commonly used terms. Economic concepts are often frequently used without it being possible to give a precise definition of them. For example, mergers and takeovers may not be allowed to proceed unless they are 'in the public interest', but this phrase is very difficult to define in practice. Even the meaning of the term 'money supply' is subject to much debate.

4. Explain why it is difficult to find a single definition for the term 'small firm'.

APPLYING ECONOMIC PRINCIPLES

1. Refer to all the Figures. (**a**) What definitions of the size of units/firms are used in the data? (**b**) Under what circumstances would you choose each of the definitions as a good indicator of size? Explain your answer. (**c**) Why might the difficulties of identifying and defining small firms present problems for policy makers?

2. Refer to Figure 18.1. (**a**) What percentage of all manufacturing units employed fewer than 100 employees? (**b**) How do the following manufacturing industries compare with this figure (**i**) motor vehicle manufacture; (**ii**) instrument engineering? (**c**) Explain the reasons for the size differences identified in (**b**). (**d**) List one other industry similar to (**b**) (**i**) and one similar to (**b**) (**ii**) in terms of the distribution of manufacturing units by size.

3. (**a**) What is meant by 'internal economies of scale'? (**b**) List three internal economies of scale that would not be available to a small, independently-owned baker's shop. (**c**) Why do small, independently owned baker's shops continue to exist when their products are also produced by very large companies? (**d**) Small retailers often join together in voluntary chains to buy from a common wholesaler. How does this help to ensure the survival of many small retailers?

4. Small firms serve limited markets. (**a**) What is meant by a 'limited market'? (**b**) Why do many very small firms exist in the engineering industry? (**c**) With reference to Figure 17.3, explain how small firms may be able to operate more efficiently than large firms in the service sector.

5. (**a**) Draw a cost curve diagram to illustrate a situation in which a small firm operates more efficiently than a large one. (**b**) What reasons may there be to explain the situation shown in your answer to (**a**)?

6. Small firms are said to be more responsive to market forces than larger firms. (**a**) Why are smaller firms able to respond more quickly to changes in market demand than larger firms? (**b**) Give one example of a manufacturing industry where small firms would be expected to survive because rapid responses to changes in the market are vital to sucess.

7. (**a**) With reference to Figure 18.3, explain why the Government might wish to support the small firm sector. (**b**) What form might such policies take?

8. (**a**) Draw a diagram to show a firm and industry in perfect competition in long-run equilibrium. Show a fall in demand on the diagram. (**b**) Under what circumstances would the firm shown in your diagram (**i**) cease production in the short run, (**ii**) close down in the long run? (**c**) To what extent might the model of perfect competition explain the pricing policy of an estate agent in a high street with many rival agencies?

FOR FURTHER INVESTIGATION
Make a study of a small firm in your area. Collect data on the product made/service provided, the nature of the market, the aims of the owner, and the type of business organization. Where appropriate, include details about pricing policy, costs and revenues, and government incentives available to the business. Write a report which uses the data and economic analysis to assess the strengths and weaknesses of the firm.

ESSAYS
Refer to the data wherever possible, especially in the first essay.

1. (**a**) What is meant by a 'small firm'? (**b**) In which sectors of the economy are small firms most common, and why?

2. Explain why large firms can produce at lower costs than small firms. Under what circumstances might the reverse be true? Illustrate your answers with examples.
[London 6/87]

The urge to merge

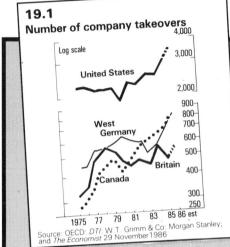

19.1
Number of company takeovers

Log scale

United States

West Germany

Canada

Britain

Source: OECD; *DTI*; W.T. Grimm & Co; Morgan Stanley; and *The Economist* 29 November 1986

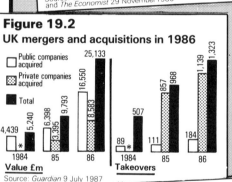

Figure 19.2
UK mergers and acquisitions in 1986

□ Public companies acquired
▨ Private companies acquired
■ Total

Value £m

Takeovers

Source: *Guardian* 9 July 1987

Figure 19.3

A head on Guinness

The strategy for improvement of Mr Saunders (chairman of Guinness) concentrated on four main areas: drinks (still only beer in those days); retailing; health products and services; and publishing (based mostly on the Guinness Book of Records, whose 2m sales each year are exceeded only by the Bible).

Having sold many of the businesses bought by his predecessors, Mr Saunders embarked on his acquisitions. Between June 1984 and August 1985, Guinness spent £98m buying a string of shop groups specialising in newspapers and magazines, confectionery and tobacco. Guinness now has 1,400 such shops—more than any other British retailer. It also owns 100 chemists through Drummonds group and 53 7-Eleven convenience stores.

In 1985, retailing (plus a few related bits and bobs) accounted for 29% of total sales but only 14% (or £13.8m) of the group's operating profits. That reflects the fact that retailing margins of 4% are only half those that Guinness has achieved on beer (7.9% in 1985, compared with only 5% in 1981).

The change of direction pleased analysts in the City of London. Guinness's sales were growing by a compound aver-

age rate of 7%, profits after-tax by 27.4% and earnings per share by 28.1%. But 1985 sales were still too narrowly based: two-thirds of the company's sales were made in Britain and Ireland, with beer accounting for roughly the same proportion. This was mirrored in its profits: 83% came from beer, and 67% from Britain and Ireland. Mr Saunders reasoned that for Guinness to break with its past it would not only have to acquire new drinks businesses but also to become more international.

During 1985, Mr Saunders had run a slide rule over Distillers, which was losing market share despite its best-selling whisky brands, such as Johnnie Walker, Dewar's White Label, White Horse, Black and White, Haig and Vat 69. With flat profits, Distillers looked vulnerable to takeover but

Guinness and its advisers felt the company (then capitalised at £1 billion) was too big to swallow whole. Mr Saunders looked for something more digestible. He found it in Arthur Bell, a whisky distiller and hotel group, that he acquired in a contested takeover in August 1985 for £410m. The purchase of Bell added annual (1984) sales of £318m and profits after tax of £41.9m. Overnight, Guinness boosted its overall sales by 28% and nearly doubled its net profits.

The results for the six months to March 31 1986 show the effects of its acquisitions. Beer fell to 48% of total sales and 46% of operating profits. Bell's contributed 21% of sales and 29% of profits. From only 15% in 1984, retailing accounted for 31% of the enlarged group's sales, and 17% of its profits.

Source: *The Economist* 4 October 1986

Main acquisitions		Cost £m
Bell Group		
Arthur Bell & Sons		
Gleneagles Hotel	August 1985	410
Canning Town Glass		
British retailing		
Martin the Newsagent	June 1984	46
Neighbourhood Stores	February 1985	16
Lewis Meeson	July 1985	5
R. S. McColl	August 1985	26
Other businesses		
Champneys Group	November 1984	3
Nature's Best Health Products	January 1985	2
Richter Brothers	February 1985	18
Hediard SA	August 1985	5

Figure 19.4

The bell tolls for takeovers

IS THE takeover boom all over, or is it merely in abeyance? If it is likely to start again once the hue and cry over insider dealing, share price manipulation and the Guinness slush fund dies down, should public policy be changed to exercise tougher control of mergers?

There is no doubt that the public climate for takeovers has shifted dramatically, as Sir Owen Green of BTR discovered when he pulled out of the battle for Pilkingtons. Big no longer means beautiful, and ministers are happy to encourage a period of quiet consolidation around the City boardrooms this side of an election.

Nevertheless have the fundamental factors which spurred takeover activity really changed? A look at the reasons why private companies merge would suggest not, so that the merry-go-round might start again. Firms may be able to reduce their joint tax bill if one of them has offsets against corporation tax it is unable to use. There are still firms which can do so.

Firms may give themselves greater

market power, and hence be able to push up prices and make larger profits for a given level of cost: nothing has changed, there is plenty of scope left for the growth of monopolies, if the competition policy allows it.

One firm may have a management team which is genuinely better than the other one, and is anxious to test its mettle on a bigger field. Thus the sum of the parts may genuinely be larger than if they remained separate. Another permanent reason for mergers is if the two firms can reap economies of scale in production or by cutting overheads. New opportunities for such economies may also arise due to technological change.

There may be financial gains merely by diversifying out of a business which is, for example, particularly cyclical or concentrated in vulnerable foreign markets. Thus the combined entity may be able to borrow more cheaply, and hence reduce the financial costs of its operations.

There may also, in the words of two coy researchers, be "information asym-

metries" — not all of them dishonest insider dealing. The bidder may have perfectly honest information about the victim not available to other market participants and hence not reflected in the market price of the victim. This is probably an important reason for agreed mergers, which are still the vast bulk of takeover activity.

"Thus Hanson Trust was able to recoup almost two thirds of the costs of acquiring the Imperial Group through subsequent sales (including Courage) whilst retaining subsidiaries which accounted for 55 per cent of Imperial's profits," say Professor Brian Chiplin and Dr Mike Wright.

There may also be, in the case of financial conglomerates, some sort of "bicycle effect": their past growth encourages the stock market to award them high share prices relative to the rest of the market. Thus their price is high relative to earnings, reflecting future expectations of more earnings.

Source: Christopher Huhne, *Guardian* 19 February 1987

Figure 19.1
Log scales are sometimes used instead of conventional scales. Occasionally the vertical scale on a graph will be shown as a 'log scale'. On a conventional vertical scale (i.e. one not using a log scale), where 'years' is on the horizontal axis, an upward-sloping straight line would show a constant absolute increase and a falling percentage increase in a value. Where a log scale is used an upward-sloping straight line would indicate a constant percentage increase. Log scales are useful, therefore, for showing the percentage change in a value from year to year.

1. Did the USA have about twice as many takeovers as Britain in 1978? Explain your answer.

2. Between 1975 and 1978, was the absolute increase in the number of takeovers in the UK more or less constant from year to year? Explain your answer.

Figure 19.2
A distinction may need to be made between volume and value. Volume refers to the quantity of something, e.g. the number of houses built in a year. Value refers to the money value of a given quantity, e.g. if one million houses are built in a year, selling at an average price of £100,000 each, then the value of the houses is £100 billion.

3. In 1986 what was (a) the number of takeovers of UK public companies, and (b) the value of UK public companies acquired?

4. What was the average value of each UK public company acquired in 1986?

Figure 19.3
Presenting information in tabular or diagrammatic form may help to summarize the main points in documentary data. Books, magazines and articles often discuss complex economic events in a descriptive manner. They may also follow through a thread of economic argument from one point to another. It is often advisable when confronted with such data to try and summarize the processes described in a flow chart graph, or table, to help clarify the major events or logical sequence of points that are being described.

5. In addition to the table shown, write one other table using information from the passage.

Figure 19.4
Newspaper and magazine articles can contain many economic points without using technical economic terms. Commentators on economic events will normally be trained in economics, but they will not want to blind their readers by using the jargon of the subject in articles intended for general readership. Even though they do not use the 'correct' technical words and terms, however, they will still express economic ideas using other language. It is important to be able to identify the economic ideas used in articles intended for general readership.

6. Which paragraphs in the article may be taken to be referring to (a) abnormal profit, and (b) managerial economies of scale?

APPLYING ECONOMIC PRINCIPLES

1. (a) Describe the trends in merger and takeover activity in Britain shown in Figures 19.1 and 19.2. (b) With reference to Figure 19.4, suggest possible reasons for these trends. (c) According to Figure 19.4, was the trend set to continue after 1987? Give reasons for your answer.

2. An advantage of integration is often quoted as economies of scale: (a) With reference to Figure 19.3, what economies of scale could have arisen from the Guinness takeover of Arthur Bell? (b) What economies of scale are identified in Figure 19.4 as possible reasons for integration?

3. A firm takes over another firm and proceeds to divest itself of unprofitable parts of the business, including closing down factories in the north-east of England. (a) What name would be given to this process by (i) the firm, and (ii) opponents of the takeover? (b) What would be (i) the private benefits, and (ii) the external costs of the process?

4. Horizontal and vertical integration can reduce competition and increase the market power of firms. (a) With reference to Figure 19.3, suggest what barriers of entry might

Guinness be able to take advantage of as a result of its acquisitions. (b) Explain the possible effect of such barriers on costs and prices.

5. (a) Draw a standard monopoly diagram showing marginal cost, average cost, marginal revenue and average revenue curves. Indicate the price and output situation if (i) the industry was a unitary monopoly, and (ii) the industry was broken up into a perfectly competitive market. (b) Explain how consumers might suffer as a result of increased monopoly power in a market. (c) Explain how consumers might benefit from the monopolization of a competitive market.

6. Under what circumstances might the government (a) approve, and (b) disapprove of integration between two British firms producing beers, wines and spirits?

7. (a) What is meant by 'industrial concentration'? (b) What effect on industrial concentration would you expect the trend shown in Figure 19.2 to have? (c) What are the possible economic effects of such a change in concentration?

FOR FURTHER INVESTIGATION
Large takeover and merger proposals are widely reported in the media. For example, the proposed British Aerospace takeover of the Rover Group in 1988 was the main story in the news for several days. Collect articles on the next major takeover or merger to be announced. Imagine that you were advising the Department of Trade and Industry about whether the takeover or merger should go ahead. Write a report outlining the advantages and disadvantages of the takeover or merger for the UK consumer and the UK economy. Conclude with a recommendation about whether the evidence suggests that the takeover or merger is in the public interest.

ESSAYS
Refer to the data wherever possible, especially in the first essay.

1. (a) To what extent was there a takeover and merger boom in the UK in the mid-1980s? (b) What factors might account for general increases or decreases in merger activity?

2. Assess the extent to which (a) horizontal mergers, and (b) vertical mergers suppress competition and act against the public interest. [Oxford 6/85]

Around the world

Figure 20.1
ICI: Turnover and trading profit for companies located in principal geographic areas

United Kingdom

£m Turnover				£m Trading profit			
	2500	5000	7500		250	500	750
1982				1982			
1983				1983			
1984				1984			
1985				1985			
1986				1986			

Continental Europe

£m Turnover				£m Trading profit			
	2500	5000	7500		250	500	750
1982				1982			
1983				1983			
1984				1984			
1985				1985			
1986				1986			

The Americas

£m Turnover				£m Trading profit			
	2500	5000	7500		250	500	750
1982				1982			
1983				1983			
1984				1984			
1985				1985			
1986				1986			

Australasia, Japan and the Far East

£m Turnover				£m Trading profit			
	2500	5000	7500		250	500	750
1982				1982			
1983				1983			
1984				1984			
1985				1985			
1986				1986			

Source: ICI *Annual Report* 1986

Figure 20.2

Multinational companies and the UK economy: recent trends

Many of the giant firms that dominate the UK economy are multinational companies. Among the best known are Ford, General Motors, ICI, and GEC. It is important to distinguish between foreign-based multinationals (e.g. Ford and General Motors) undertaking inward investment and production in the UK, and UK-based multinationals (e.g. ICI and GEC) undertaking outward investment and production abroad.

Recent trends in the changing impact of multinationals on the UK economy have occurred within the context of global trends. Initially, firms such as Ford set up their overseas operations simply to gain a foothold in important overseas markets, and these operations would form part of a separate overseas division. Since the late 1960s and especially more recently, overseas operations have assumed greater significance as part of *global* corporate strategy, with production and investment in different sectors and at different stages being shifted around in accordance with global profit maximization. This has, in turn, led to more widespread national origins. For example, five of the world's top 200 multinational industrial companies are now based in South Korea. While the US still produces 57 per cent of the total sales of these 200 companies, this compares with 73 per cent in 1960.

With the increasing globalization of capital, there has been a greater variety of directions of investment. Up to the 1960s the direction was mainly from the US to Europe. Since then, European and Japanese firms have invested increasingly in the US, and newly industrialized countries, such as Brazil, Taiwan and South Korea, have assumed greater importance as targets for multinational companies' investment. European and US multinationals are now also looking towards Japan for high rates of return, despite Japanese government restrictions.

Diversification by multinational companies has also occurred. Originally, the bulk of their operations were capital intensive in relatively technically advanced areas of manufacturing. Since the 1960s multinationals have spread to non-manufacturing sectors, such as construction, property, shipping, retailing and especially banking and finance, where some multinational companies' development of their own banking and financial operations has parallelled the increasing internationalization of the large banks as a whole.

Source: *British Economy Survey* Autumn 1985

Figure 20.3

Multinationals & the failure of economic management

The cash flows of the multinational corporation are replacing oil revenues as the determinants of currency markets. As few as 20 to 30 companies worldwide, dominated by oil, car, and chemical corporations, are powerful enough to move the foreign exchange markets through their currency dealings. Companies can also avoid exchange controls by accepting international payments in the form of goods, which can then be traded elsewhere, and so on.

The international web of equity, lending and currency markets is a boggling complex of wheeler-dealing. The domination by a few leading banks and corporations with massive resources makes macroeconomic policies aimed at the regulation of exchange rates and interest rates look like the proverbial shuffling of deckchairs on the Titanic.

The reality of the British economy is one of dominance where the performance of a few giant corporations determines all others. The second reality is that the current armoury of instruments is ineffective when applied to the giant corporations in the real and money economies. Clearly, domestic monetary restrictions are of little consequence to giant corporations who can operate on international money markets. Multinational corporations have considerable flexibility for moving their funds around the globe — often electronically — to circumvent any form of control.

Money is so internationally fluid that exchange and interest rates cannot be easily controlled or effectively used as policy instruments. Only policies that directly control the biggest companies allow for a national policy for growth. This means taking a stake in multinational industrial and financial corporations.

Source: *British Economy Survey* Autumn 85

Figure 20.1

It may be misleading to use a single indicator to assess a firm's performance. Economic theory suggests that firms try to maximize total profit (i.e. total revenue minus total costs). In the real world firms make use of a range of indicators to assess performance, of which profit is just one. When examining statistics about a firm, a range of data should be considered to determine whether the firm is performing adequately. Often additional data, not directly related to the firm in question, would be useful in assessing how well a firm is doing comparatively.

1. In what sense can it be said that the UK activities of ICI were **(a)** more successful in 1985 than 1986, **(b)** less successful in 1985 than 1986?

2. In view of the falling profits in the Americas in 1986, should ICI have considered reducing its operation in the area? Explain your answer.

Figure 20.2

New words and terms are added constantly to the vocabulary of economics. The world which economists analyse is subject to constant change, and the pace of change has quickened with the advent of microtechnology and improved communications. As a result of these changes new industries have developed and other industries have declined. National boundaries have become increasingly less significant as economic forces transcend them. New words and terms are constantly being added to the language of economics to cope with these changes, for example, 'the information technology industry' and 'multinational company'. Often it is difficult to define these new terms precisely as no official definition has been established for them.

3. Explain what is meant by **(a)** 'global corporate strategy', **(b)** 'globalization', and **(c)** 'internationalization of the large banks'.

Figure 20.3

Writers on economic affairs may hold very strong political views which are reflected in their use of language. Commentators on economic affairs are under no obligation to be 'neutral' in their views on economic events. Often the most perceptive and stimulating articles are written by economists with strong views on a particular subject. Writers may use strong language to express their views. For example, the writers of this article refer to international financial markets as 'a boggling complex of wheeler-dealing'.

4. (a) Does the passage suggest that the authors are in favour of multinationals? **(b)** Write out two phrases or sentences, apart from the one already mentioned, that support your answer.

APPLYING ECONOMIC PRINCIPLES

1. (a) Use the data in Figure 20.1 to explain why ICI is called a multinational. **(b)** Calculate whether the UK contributed to the majority of ICI's turnover in 1986. **(c) (i)** For what reasons might ICI be increasing its involvement overseas? **(ii)** What problems could this cause for ICI?

2. Refer to Figure 20.2. **(a)** What two types of multinationals are mentioned in the article? **(b)** Why did firms like Ford initially begin production outside their country of origin? **(c)** What motive accounts for the fact that multinationals are now willing to switch their operations from country to country? **(d)** How have capital movements changed since the 1960s with the growth of multinationals? **(e)** How have multinationals diversified their activities in recent years?

3. Refer to Figure 20.3. **(a)** What power have the 20 or 30 giant oil, car and chemical companies got that so concerns the authors of the article? **(b)** Name two financial markets which the multinationals may now dominate as a result of their economic power. **(c) (i)** What does the article suggest that governments should consider doing to control the multinationals? **(ii)** What are the possible economic costs and benefits of such policies?

4. Assess the implications of multinational involvement in the car industry in the UK for: **(a)** workers; **(b)** consumers; **(c)** the Rover Group.

5. (a) Why might an electronics firm decide to close a factory in an industrialized country like the UK and open a factory in a developing country such as Taiwan or South Korea? **(b)** What advantages and disadvantages might this have for: **(i)** workers in the developing country? **(ii)** consumers in the world market? **(c)** Why do some trade unions in the UK object to the import of goods made by multinationals in developing countries?

6. How can the following contribute towards global profit maximization? **(a)** The adoption of different specifications in different markets. **(b)** The deliberate making of a loss in one particular region.

FOR FURTHER INVESTIGATION

Many multinationals make their annual reports freely available, and they often produce other information for the public. Try to obtain copies of the annual report, and any other available information, for three multinational companies. List their areas of operation and the regions in which they produce. In the face of public criticism multinationals often try to justify their activities in their literature. Using the information you have collected, write a short account of the benefits that multinationals claim to provide for their customers and their workers.

ESSAYS

Refer to the data wherever possible, especially in the first essay.

1. (a) What is meant by 'a multinational company'? **(b)** Why do large companies tend to operate increasingly on an international basis? **(c)** What advantages and disadvantages exist for developing economies that are subject to increasing multinational activity?

2. 'Multinationals are outside the control of governments therefore they have no need to take regard of external costs when planning their operations.' Discuss.

A question of capital

Figure 21.1
British Industries' net sources of finance

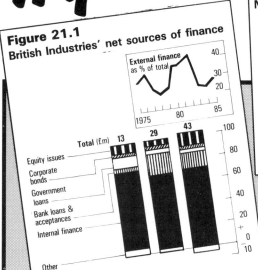

Source: CSO and *The Economist* 7 June 1986

Figure 21.2
New issues by UK companies by type of security

	Debt				Preference		Ordinary		Total issues
	Convertible debt £m	Other debt £m	Total debt £m	% of total issues	£m	% of total issues	£m	% of total issues	£m
1971-5 (average)	71.5	115.4	186.9	26.2	16.5	2.3	510.8	71.5	714.2
1976-80 (av.)	52.3	42.4	94.7	9.9	38.3	4.0	819.8	86.0	952.7
1981	373.5	66.9	440.4	16.5	113.1	4.2	2,110.8	79.2	2,664.3
1982	71.3	944.8	1,016.1	45.9	32.5	1.5	1,165.4	52.6	2,214.0
1983	64.4	461.1	525.5	17.7	80.7	2.7	2,370.1	79.6	2,976.3
1984	118.1	1,043.6	1,161.7	36.4	78.4	2.5	1,947.5	61.1	3,187.7
1985	328.5	2,266.2	2,594.7	32.4	455.2	5.7	4,962.3	61.9	8,012.1

Source: *Midland Bank Review* Spring, 1986

Figure 21.3

External finance

Despite their greatly improved financial position, companies' appetite for external finance has been undiminished, typically accounting for around 30 per cent of total sources of funds during the 1980s, close to the long-run average. However, within this, balance sheets have been transformed because the recovery of profits has promoted buoyant stock market conditions which, in turn, have enabled companies to supplement retained earnings with rights issues; this shift from debt to equity has been encouraged by the progressive reduction of corporate tax rates. The past two years have seen companies raise record amounts from ordinary share issues: £3.4 billion in 1985 and £5 billion in 1986.

On the debt side, although there has been something of a revival in corporate bond issues, the increase in new bank borrowing by industrial and commercial companies appears fairly high, averaging about £6.5 billion over the last three years. However, expressed as a proportion of total external finance, gross bank borrowing has fallen from almost 80 per cent to just under 40 per cent over the past two years, well below the long-run average and although in inflation-adjusted terms, gross bank borrowing has remained considerably above 1960s levels, this is not the case in net terms, (ie after making due allowance for the build-up of bank deposits). Indeed, during two of the past four years, the corporate sector has been a net supplier of funds to the banking system, and on a far larger scale than in the past, thus bringing about a reduction in its net debt and a corresponding increase in corporate liquidity.

Source: *Barclays Bank Review* May 1987

Figure 21.4

The Euro-equity market

The world's various equity (share) markets have traditionally been distinct and national. On the Paris Bourse, the French bought shares in Peugot, while on the Zurich Stock Exchange, the Swiss bought Nestlé. These markets were usually situated in big buildings, where men scurried about the trading floor excitedly buying and selling shares.

The Eurobond market is different from these national stockmarkets. When a company issues bonds, it borrows money from investors at a fixed annual rate of interest and for a fixed period, after which it has to repay the debt. But when a company sells equities to investors, the bits of paper represent not debt, but a share in the ownership of the company. An equity is never repaid, and its holder receives a dividend which varies with the performance of the company.

The Eurobond market is international. Eurobonds are issued by borrowers and bought by investors from all countries. The Eurobond market has no trading floor. Traders watch screens to see the latest prices, and buy and sell by telephone and telex. Most of the banks in the Eurobond market are in London, but because of the absence of a trading floor the geographical location of the market is largely arbitrary.

In the past two years, the character of the world's equity markets has grown closer to that of the Eurobond market. Companies have started to distribute their new share issues globally, through syndicates of international banks. Because this technique in the "primary" equity market (ie, the issuing of new shares rather than the trading of existing ones, which is called the secondary market) is similar to the way new Eurobonds are sold, bankers have dubbed this the Euro-equity market.

The trading of equities has also become more international. Shares of ICI, a British chemicals multinational, are bought and sold in New York. Big blocks of shares in Japan's Sony and West Germany's Allianz are traded in London—far from their home markets. About 500 shares are now traded actively in more than one centre. Shares traded away from their country of origin are known as international equities—or sometimes Euro-equities. International equities are traded in London in the same way as Eurobonds, "over-the-counter"—ie, not on a trading floor.

Nobody has measured total international equity trading in London. But the American Securities Industry Association reckons that in 1985 the gross transaction volume of American equity trading (sales and purchases) in London amounted to $38 billion. That is half the comparable volume of equity trading on the London Stock Exchange. If international trading of non-American stock in London was added, volume would probably match the London Stock Exchange.

Source: *The Economist* 29 November 1986

Figure 21.1
Percentage shares in a bar chart may not be easily identified.
Bar charts are often difficult to interpret. On some occasions, as in the ones shown here, the bar will represent 100 per cent of a total figure. In such a case it is important to measure the percentage share of a portion of a bar chart between the starting and finishing points of the portion rather than between the origin and the finishing point.

1. What happened to government loans as a source of finance between 1980 and 1985 (**a**) in percentage terms, and (**b**) in absolute terms?

2. For what reasons might the bar for 1985 reach above 100 per cent at the top and below 0 per cent at the bottom?

Figure 21.2
Averages for particular periods and figures for specific years may be used in the same data. Occasionally statistics will give data for periods covering a number of years, as well as for individual years. Long period averages can mask large fluctuations within the period and they should be treated with caution. For example, a five-year average for an exchange rate would be of little use for the 1970s and 1980s because exchange rates were so volatile: a five-year average for the 1950s would be more useful because exchange rates were stable under an adjustable peg system.

3. (**a**) What was the average value of total security issues between 1971 and 1975? (**b**) What was the average value of total security issues between 1981 and 1985?

4. With reference to the individual years between 1981 and 1985, explain why such averages may not be very meaningful.

Figure 21.3
Terms may have different meanings in different contexts. Economics has its own vocabulary, and many of the words and terms used may have somewhat different, or completely different, meanings in different contexts. For example, 'capital' may refer in some contexts to the finance required to purchase capital goods, and in other contexts to the capital goods themselves.

5. (**a**) What is meant by 'long-run average' in Figure 21.3? (**b**) What is meant by 'long-run' in the context of (**i**) the economic theory of production, (**ii**) the classical theory of the firm?

Figure 21.4
Important distinctions are often blurred. Textbooks often make very clear distinctions between different categories, whereas in articles in newspapers and magazines these distinctions may be less clearly made. For example, newspaper articles may refer to a takeover as a 'merger', implying incorrectly that two firms have integrated on a more or less equal basis. It is also not always clear whether 'trade' figures reported in newspapers refer to the Balance of Trade or the Current Account Balance.

6. (**a**) What is the difference between a 'primary' and 'secondary' market? (**b**) Write one sentence or phrase which indicates that the Eurobond market is partly a primary market, and one sentence or phrase which indicates that it is partly a secondary market.

APPLYING ECONOMIC PRINCIPLES

1. When finance is provided for a firm, the firm will be required to reward the individual or organization providing the finance. The reward can take the form of 'dividends' or 'interest'. Use examples from Figures 21.1 and 21.2 to illustrate your answers to the following questions. (**a**) Under what circumstances is a 'dividend' paid by a firm, and under what circumstances is 'interest' paid by a firm? (**b**) (**i**) What types of share can be issued by a large company? (**ii**) Which shareholders receive a variable dividend and which receive a fixed dividend? (**c**) Why do large companies issue such a variety of securities?

2. Refer to Figures 21.1 and 21.3. (**a**) What is the difference between 'internal' and 'external' finance? (**b**) (**i**) What proportion of company finance was internal in 1985? (**ii**) For what reasons might companies prefer internal finance? (**c**) (**i**) What happened to financing by bank lending between 1982 and 1986? (**ii**) What happened to financing by equity issue in 1985 and 1986? (**iii**) Why might companies prefer equity issue to bank lending as a source of finance? (**d**) (**i**) What is meant by 'gearing'? (**ii**) Refer to Figures 21.2 and 21.3 and explain what was likely to have happened to firms' gearing in 1985. Give reasons for your answer.

3. Refer to Figures 21.1, 21.2 and 21.3. (**a**) What percentage of total firms' financing came in 1975 and in 1985 from (**i**) security issues, (**ii**) equity issue? (**b**) What exogenous factors might account for a much higher debt to equity issue in some years rather than others?

4. Refer to Figure 21.4. (**a**) What major change has there been in recent years in the geographical location of the sources of finance for large firms? (**b**) What technological changes have made this change possible? (**c**) In what ways might capital markets be said to be becoming more 'perfect'?

FOR FURTHER INVESTIGATION
Banks provide a range of services to assist firms, and the information about such services is easily available. Try to obtain some literature from commercial banks on the financing facilities available to business, and also look in the newspapers for relevant advertisements. Write a report for an imaginary new firm describing how they can use commercial banks to finance their business.

ESSAYS
Refer to the data wherever possible, especially in the first essay.
1. (**a**) How might large companies raise finance for a major capital investment project? (**b**) Assess the advantages and disadvantages of the main methods of finance for the company involved.
2. Discuss the impact of recent changes in capital markets for (**a**) large companies, (**b**) the City of London.

The Big Bang

Figure 22.1

The benefits of the Big Bang

Big Bang brought considerable changes to the City. It has meant price competition and freedom of access for new entrants and capital. Specialisation in the provision of security dealing has given way to diversification. The main dealers and brokers are now the subsidiaries of large domestic and international financial conglomerates. The market has adopted a modern screen-based dealing system and largely abandoned the traditional central market place, but the new technology does enable London to participate fully in the trading of global securities. The recent merger of the Stock Exchange and ISRO assures London of a major role in the Golden Triangle of security dealing, along with New York and Tokyo.

For the investor the changes have produced lower transaction costs. Commissions have fallen, as have the dealing margins of market-makers. Also, the recent changes have brought a great surge of facilities with participants vying with each other to attract the custom of investors, large and small. But the protection of single capacity against conflicts of interests has been eroded. While the market is more visible, the investor is left to rely more on self-protection. In the background the regulatory framework has been stiffened by legislation with the creation of the Securities Investment Board and its satellite Self-Regulatory Organisations.

Borrowers will also see gains. The gilt-edged market with its numerous well-capitalised dealers now offers the authorities a more robust arena in which to make new issues and contemplate new practices. In the equity market there are prospects for changing the way in which shares are brought to the market, leading to lower costs and greater flexibility. These large changes have been introduced in what is a remarkably short period.

Source: *The Economic Review* May 1987

Figure 22.2

A foreign City?

Keeping the City in British hands will not be easy. Only eight of the City's top 20 stockbroking firms have maintained their British nationality in the recent rash of acquisitions. It will be left to these and British banks to carry the flag. Eight of London's 16 Accepting Houses (merchant banks), and three of the four clearing banks, have joined the auction for market share in equities and gilts after Big Bang abolishes fixed commission on October 27th. Vying with foreign banks and securities houses, they have bought broking and jobbing firms, and are growing talent inhouse or hiring it.

Three years ago, the City was as British as John Bull. It was also a cartel. Commercial banks dominated the bank-loan market, merchant banks were the prima donnas of corporate finance, stockbrokers acted as agents for debt and equity investors, and jobbers had a monopoly on market-making in securities. To cap it all, commissions on securities broking were fixed at an average of roughly one-third the rate in New York. Foreigners took the lead in the (far bigger) markets for Eurobonds and foreign exchange, but were banned from membership of the London Stock Exchange and hence from trading in British equities and gilts on the floor of the exchange.

Today, fewer than 20 British institutions of any size are still there.

Source: *The Economist* 30 August 1986

Figures 22.3

The financial services conglomerate of the future

A global institution formed around existing individual entities, such as commercial and merchant banks, stock/insurance brokers, jobbers and licensed dealers.

Money transmission	Personal lending	Business lending	Insurance	New issues	Investment advice and Securities trading	Foreign currency dealings and international settlements
e.g. cheque encashment, settlement and clearance	e.g. provision of finance for house and consumer durables purchase	e.g. provision of working capital through secured and unsecured lending	(broking and policy writing)	(provision of longer-term finance for corporations through debt and shares)	(for private and institutional investors)	
					'In-house' capital market	
Domestic					Domestic and International	International

Source: *Economics* Autumn 1986

Figure 22.4

Bloodbath: Jobbers opt out

AS SHARE prices crashed yet again on Friday, criticism mounted over the refusal of the Stock Exchange's new style market-makers to make a proper market.

Stockbrokers, attempting to sell shares for clients, claimed that leading market-makers were refusing to answer their telephones and make a market in the shares which they are supposed to trade in.

Criticism of the lack of liquidity in the Stock Exchange's new electronic marketplace gathered momentum throughout last week's equity bloodbath.

Stockbrokers complained that, although market-makers were making a price on the Stock Exchange's SEAQ screens, they were not, in reality, carrying out transactions.

Major City market-makers, including Barclays de Zoete Wedd and Warburgs, were widely criticised on this account.

In the words of one senior stockbroker: 'If they want to call themselves market-makers, they should make markets. We have been constantly telephoning firms to no avail. It is disgraceful practice and, as usual, the Stock Exchange has done nothing about it.'

A spokesman for the Stock Exchange said yesterday: 'We only received one complaint on this count on Friday. If stockbrokers find they cannot deal with a market-maker, they should report the matter to our Supervisory Committee.

But the City remains something of a club, and stockbrokers are inevitably loath to report a market-maker to the Stock Exchange Tower—not least because of the threat of receiving unfavourable treatment when they attempt to do business with the market-maker in the future.

According to one critic: 'Can you imagine the spread that would be made by a market-maker whom you had reported.'

He added: 'All the Stock Exchange's supervisory personnel need to do is pick up a telephone and attempt to make contact with the market-makers. It has been pandemonium today. There is no real market.'

The inability of stockbrokers to 'get on' during Friday's £7 billion share slide represents the most serious criticism of the Stock Exchange's marketplace to date.

In the wake of last October's Big Bang revolution, the City has witnessed a one-way bull market.

But Thursday's unexpected one-point rise in base rates to 10 per cent has heralded a significant reversal in sentiment and, under selling pressure, the Stock Exchange's market-making procedures have proved wanting.

When dealings were carried out on the traditional Stock Exchange floor, 'jobbers' had no choice other than to deal at the prices marked on the board. Under the new system, the telephone provides the market-maker with an effective shield against selling orders.

High level complaints concerning the market's illiquidity on Thursday and Friday—when the FT-SE Index fell 91 points—are expected to be delivered privately from certain senior stockbrokers to Sir Nicholas Goodison, chairman of the Stock Exchange.

If the City's market-makers continue to fight shy of taking stock on their books London's image as a financial centre will inevitably suffer—not least in the eyes of Wall Street and Tokyo.

The impact on share prices of domino-style inter market-maker dealing is also causing concern.

Source: *Observer* 9 August 1987

Figure 22.1
Newspaper and magazine articles may refer implicitly rather than explicitly to economic theory. Economists will often write about a subject from the point of view of a particular set of economic ideas or theories. These economic ideas and theories may not be explicitly mentioned, however. For example, articles on fluctuating oil prices may in fact be about the conditions of supply and demand, and why equilibrium price is so difficult to reach in the market: none of the economic terms may be mentioned directly by name.

1. Which area of economic theory may have been in the writer's mind when he or she wrote the second sentence? Give reasons for your answer.

Figure 22.2
Newspaper and magazine articles may implicitly rather than explicitly make assumptions about what is desirable. Commentators on economic events frequently have a point of view about the desirability or undesirability of some economic event. For example, many writers in the UK may welcome the moves by the Soviet Union to increase the use of market forces in the Soviet economy. The writers will rarely make a statement such as 'an economy based on the use of markets is more desirable than a centrally planned economy'. This view can only be inferred from the article.

2. What appears to be the writer's view about the increasing internationalization of the City of London? Give evidence for your answer.

Figure 22.3
Economic institutions are becoming increasingly internationalized. The reduction of barriers to trade in both goods and services, increasing world trade, and improvements in communications, have reduced the isolation of individual economies. Business and finance are becoming dominated by multinational companies who produce and distribute throughout the world. This trend is becoming increasingly evident in data which relate to the new institutions which are developing, especially in the field of global finance.

3. Explain what is meant by 'a global institution formed around existing individual entities'.

Figure 22.4
Newspapers often use emotive words to emphasise points made. Newspapers have to making their leading news articles lively and interesting, even if they 'go over the top'. Often emotive words which may seem deliberately out of place in the particular context are used to give emphasis. Newspapers will also tend to report the views of 'sources' who have very strong feelings on a particular topic, even if the majority of people involved in the event take less extreme views.

4. List two emotive words used to describe the situation in the stock market following the large fall in share prices.

APPLYING ECONOMIC PRINCIPLES

1. Refer to Figure 22.1 to answer (b), (c) and (d). The Big Bang was intended to introduce more competition into financial markets. (a) What are the main features of a 'competitive market'? (b) What changes in the stock market introduced in the Big Bang have made it more competitive? (c) In what ways could consumers of financial services benefit from more competitive financial markets? (d) What problems could arise for consumers of financial services as a result of the Big Bang?

2. Refer to Figure 22.2. (a) Define: (i) 'acquisition', (ii) 'cartel', (iii) 'monopoly on market-making in securities'. (b) Describe the major change in the City of London that is outlined in the article. (c) To what extent could the change lead to (i) more competition, and (ii) less competition? (d) What (i) advantages, and (ii) disadvantages will arise for the UK economy as a result of the change?

3. Refer to Figure 22.3. (a) Define 'financial services conglomerate'. (b) List the separate institutions that in the past would have carried out each of the separate services now being offered by financial conglomerates. (c) What (i) advantages, and (ii) disadvantages could arise for the individual consumer of financial services as a result of the growth of large financial conglomerates?

4. Refer to Figure 22.4. (a) Define (i) 'making a proper market', and (ii) liquidity. (b) What factors appear to have prevented stockbrokers making a proper market after the fall in share prices? (c) What might have been the short-term effect on the price of shares of the failure of the market to clear quickly? (d) With reference to the last two paragraphs, what might be the longer term effect of the failure of stockbrokers to make a proper market?

FOR FURTHER INVESTIGATION
Keep an account of share prices over a period of a month or more and record your findings on a graph. Newspapers, radio and television give frequent accounts about share price changes. List the factors that affect share prices and indicate important individual factors on your graph, e.g. an interest rate rise which usually depresses share prices. Write a short report on the factors that have affected share prices in the period that you have studied.

ESSAYS
1. (a) Describe the major changes in the organization of financial markets in the City of London in recent years. (b) Explain how the changes will enable the stock market to become more competitive.
2. To what extent has the stock market a life of its own, divorced from the production of real goods and services?

23 Trade unions

What about the workers?

Figure 23.1
Trade unions: their numbers and membership

per cent

	1974	1975	1976	1977	1978	1979	1980	1981	1982	1983	1984	1985
Number of trade unions	507	501	473	481	462	453	438	414	407	394	375	373
Analysis by number of members:												
Under 100 members	15.8	16.0	14.6	15.4	15.6	16.1	15.8	17.1	19.1	17.8	18.1	19.8
100 and under 500	27.2	27.5	30.2	30.1	29.2	27.4	26.9	28.0	24.3	26.4	25.1	25.2
500 and under 1 000	10.3	10.8	9.9	9.4	10.4	10.4	10.3	9.9	11.8	10.7	10.2	9.9
1 000 and under 2 500	13.6	13.2	12.7	13.7	13.4	12.8	12.8	12.1	12.5	14.4	14.6	15.3
2 500 and under 5 000	10.3	9.0	9.5	8.5	8.0	9.5	8.9	8.9	9.3	7.9	8.6	7.0
5 000 and under 10 000	6.1	6.0	6.3	5.8	5.6	5.3	5.7	5.6	5.6	4.5	4.3	3.8
10 000 and under 15 000	2.2	2.2	1.7	2.1	1.9	1.5	1.6	1.0	0.7	0.5	0.8	1.1
15 000 and under 25 000	3.6	3.4	3.2	2.7	3.0	4.2	4.8	3.6	4.4	5.1	4.0	2.9
25 000 and under 50 000	3.4	4.0	3.6	3.7	4.1	3.3	4.3	4.1	3.7	3.8	5.1	6.2
50 000 and under 100 000	2.8	3.0	3.0	3.1	3.0	3.5	3.2	3.4	3.2	3.3	3.5	2.4
100 000 and under 250 000	2.8	2.8	3.0	3.1	3.2	3.5	3.4	3.4	2.7	2.8	3.0	3.8
250 000 and over	2.2	2.2	2.3	2.3	2.4	2.4	2.3	2.9	2.7	2.8	2.7	2.7
All sizes	100	100	100	100	100	100	100	100	100	100	100	100
Membership[3] (Thousands)												
Total	11 764	12 193	12 386	12 846	13 112	13 289	12 947	12 106	11 593	11 337	11 086	10 716
Analysis by size of union:												
Under 100 members	–	–	–	–	–	–	–	–	–	0.2	0.2	0.2
100 and under 500	0.3	0.3	0.3	0.3	0.3	0.3	0.2	0.3	0.3	0.3	0.2	0.3
500 and under 1 000	0.3	0.3	0.3	0.2	0.3	0.2	0.2	0.2	0.7	0.8	0.8	0.9
1 000 and under 2 500	0.9	0.9	0.8	0.8	1.0	1.2	1.1	1.0	1.1	1.0	1.0	1.0
2 500 and under 5 000	1.5	1.2	1.2	1.1	1.3	1.2	1.3	1.3	1.3	1.0	1.0	0.8
5 000 and under 10 000	1.7	1.6	1.6	1.4	1.3	1.2	1.3	1.3	1.3	1.0	1.0	0.4
10 000 and under 15 000	1.1	1.1	0.8	1.0	0.9	0.6	0.6	0.4	0.4	0.2	0.3	1.9
15 000 and under 25 000	2.9	2.7	2.4	2.0	2.0	2.7	3.0	2.9	3.1	3.5	2.7	7.5
25 000 and under 50 000	5.2	5.4	5.0	5.0	5.4	4.2	5.6	5.0	4.7	4.8	5.9	6.1
50 000 and under 100 000	8.1	8.6	8.0	7.9	7.2	7.6	7.9	7.9	8.4	8.5	8.8	21.9
100 000 and under 250 000	16.6	16.4	16.6	17.1	17.3	18.0	19.4	17.9	16.1	16.6	18.2	58.9
250 000 and over	61.3	61.5	62.9	63.1	63.6	63.4	59.9	62.2	63.7	63.1	60.9	100
All sizes	100	100	100	100	100	100	100	100	100	100	100	

Source: *Annual Abstract of Statistics*

Figure 23.2
Industrial disputes—working days lost: by cause; and number of stoppages

Working days lost United Kingdom Millions (30 25 20 15 10 5 0) Thousands

Legend:
- Wage disputes
- Other disputes (no figures from 1982)
- Total

Number of stoppages (4 2 0)

1961 64 67 70 73 76 79 82 84 86

Source: *Social Trends*

Figure 23.3

The future of the trade union movement

Report on a speech made to the TUC by Norman Willis, General Secretary of the TUC.

● **Services:** Referring to total union membership numbers, Mr Willis says: "With a potential market of 9.5m, we ought to be able to expand the benefits of cheap insurance, holiday schemes, car breakdown, mortgage facilities."

But he goes further, suggesting that while many union members are low paid, others in work are better paid than ever before, and often need advice, which they should be able to obtain from their unions, about the best possible pension or investing a lump sum.

He says that "like it or not, trade unionists are amongst the 5m people who've bought shares under Mrs Thatcher. That number will increase, certainly for the next four years. So they might as well have access to broking facilities provided by a trade union."

● **Women:** Accepting that for their own survival and self-interest and because they have a moral responsibility to do so, unions need to find ways of organising and representing peripheral employees such as part-time or temporary workers, Mr Willis says that many of these are women.

He says: "In future, our role must be to act as the most articulate, most persuasive, most dynamic voice of women in Britain."

Acknowledging this as "quite a challenge" for unions, he says it will pose some difficult questions about how unions allocate their resources, and says that "to be frank, as long as the majority of negotiators locally and nationally, are men then they won't always perceive the needs of women members."

● **Shop stewards:** Developing a theme he has previously mentioned, Mr Willis says that unions will have to give serious thought to re-assessing the role of shop stewards in the light of greater emphasis by companies on communications, on a sharper management style, on human resource development and on winning greater employee commitment.

He questions whether stewards should "become less of a negotiator or a rival to the boss for worker loyalty, and more of an organiser concentrating on recruitment and communication with members."

Finally, stressing a greater community role for unions, he says: "The traditional roles of unions remain, more necessary than ever. Our task is to ensure that we have the organisation, the policies and the image to carry out those roles successfully."

Source: *Financial Times* 4 August 1987

Figure 23.1

It is important to identify the main trends in complex tabulated data. Government statistical publications like the *Annual Abstract of Statistics* give a mass of detailed information about many aspects of the economy. It is important to try to identify trends and patterns in the figures and, if a written summary has to be given, use just a few figures to illustrate the points made. It is never worthwhile when analysing statistics simply to rewrite them laboriously in words without making any attempt to select figures to illustrate particular points.

1. For the year 1985, describe: (**a**) the pattern of trade union membership by size of union; (**b**) the pattern of trade unions by number of members. Use selected figures to illustrate your answers.

Figure 23.2

All the information on a graph must be taken into account when analysing the graph. When confronted with a graph it is tempting to look at the main body of information and perhaps ignore or overlook other vital information such as the heading, footnotes, or even the labelling on the axes. The correct interpretation of graphs requires a careful consideration of all the information available to avoid misunderstanding.

2. Which one of the following statements is correct for 1982?: (**a**) 'There were approximately 5 million strikes in 1982'; (**b**) 'When the time lost by each worker who stopped work due to an industrial dispute in the UK in 1982 is added up, the total comes to about five million days'; (**c**) 'The total length of all strikes in the UK in 1982 adds up to approximately 5 million days'. Explain your answer.

Figure 23.3

In analysing a speech, the objectives of the person making the speech must be considered. Newspapers and magazines frequently report the speeches of leading figures in the political and economic world. The speeches will usually have been written for a particular audience, and it is necessary for the purpose of analysing the speech to consider the motives of the speaker. For example, a speech made by the Chancellor of the Exchequer to business people may make exaggeratedly optimistic claims about the state of the economy in order to encourage more investment. A speech made by the leader of the opposition to potential voters may exaggerate economic problems to secure more votes.

3. (**a**) Who was Mr Willis's speech addressed to? (**b**) What do you think were the main aims of Mr Willis's speech?

APPLYING ECONOMIC PRINCIPLES

1. Refer to Figure 23.1. (**a**) What happened to the number of trade unionists between 1974 and 1985? Use figures to illustrate your answer. (**b**) What possible reasons could account for the trends in union membership? (**c**) What happened to the number of trade unions between 1974 and 1985? Use some figures to illustrate your answer. (**d**) What possible economic reasons are there for this trend? (**e**) Did the change in the number of unions affect the size of unions over the same period? Use figures to illustrate your answer.

2. Refer to Figure 23.2. (**a**) (**i**) In which three years were there the greatest number of days lost as a result of strikes? (**ii**) Can it be inferred from the data that when there is an increasing number of days lost in industrial disputes it is because there are more strikes? (**b**) For what reasons might more days be lost through pay disputes in some years than others? (**c**) (**i**) Between 1961 and 1982, approximately how many days were lost on average as a result of disputes that were not about pay? (**ii**) Give three possible reasons other than pay for industrial disputes.

3. Refer to Figure 23.3. (**a**) What problem, described in your answer to question 1, was Mr Willis addressing himself to in his speech? (**b**) Describe three ways in which he intended to improve the situation.

4. The government has passed legislation in recent years to try and reduce the power of the 'closed shop'. (**a**) What is a 'closed shop'. (**b**) What advantage might a closed shop agreement hold for (**i**) an employer faced with a number of unions in a factory, and (**ii**) trade unions? (**c**) Draw a demand and supply diagram to show the theoretical effect of the introduction of a closed shop on a labour market. What does economic theory predict will be the effect of this on (**i**) workers, and (**ii**) employers? (**d**) Some firms have insisted on one-union agreements before they will open a new factory. (**i**) What is a one-union agreement, and how does it differ from a closed shop? (**ii**) Why might a government approve of a one-union agreement but disapprove of a closed shop agreement? (**e**) Will one-union agreements increase productive efficiency for those firms which adopt them? Explain your answer.

FOR FURTHER INVESTIGATION

The HMSO publication, *Social Trends*, which is available at main reference libraries, carries details about union membership in individual industries. Write an analysis, supported by statistical data, to show the incidence of union membership in different industries, and how it is changing. Give reasons for the patterns and trends that you have observed.

ESSAYS

Refer to the data wherever possible, especially in the first essay.

1. (**a**) Describe and account for the relationship from 1977 to 1984 between the number of trade unionists and (**i**) the number of strikes, (**ii**) the number of working days lost as a result of strikes. (**b**) Can the trade unions ever hope to increase their membership and their power again in the future?

2. (**a**) What factors affect the ability of trade unions to increase the real wages of their members relative to other groups? (**b**) In what sense, if any, could it be argued that trade unions protect workers from 'exploitation' by employers? [Welsh 6/85]

A fair day's pay

Figure 24.1
Winners and losers in the pay stakes

Britain's Top Ten directors in public companies
(figures may include overseas earnings and bonuses)

Sir Ralph Halpern	Burton Group	£1 004 000	Nurses (1st year student)	*£4 540	Electrician	£10 920
Richard Giordano	British Oxygen Group	£772 800	Shop assistant	£4 841	University lecturer (entry age 27)	£11 014
Joseph Burnett-Stuart	Robert Flemings Holdings	£509 000	Farm labourer	£6 292	Miner	£11 819.6
Stanley Kalms	Dixons	£487 654	Butcher	£6 708	Prison officer	£15 121.6
David Scholey	Mercury Securities	£478 000	Staff nurse (newly qualified)	*£7 300	MP	£18 500
'Tiny' Rowland	Lonrho	£476 000	Teacher (newly qualified primary and secondary)	£7 881	Dentist	*£23 510
Richard Ringwald	Laporte Industries	£409 908	Van salesman	£8 257.6	NHS GP	*£27 172
Lord Rothermere	Associated Newspapers	£393 430	Motor mechanic	£8 517.6	Chairman BBC	£33 820
Denys Henderson	ICI	£393 068	Postman	£9 297.6	Prime Minister	£58 650
William Wyllie	BSR International	£380 000	Plumber	£9 672	High Court Judge	£62 100

* WITH INCREASE

Source: Charterterhouse Guide to Top Management Remuneration in the UK 1986–87, New Earnings Survey 1986, HMSO, and *Observer* 26 April 1987.

Figure 24.2
Earnings and prices

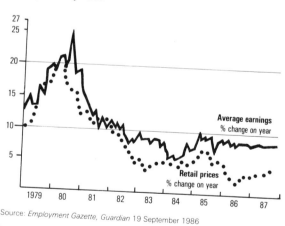

Source: *Employment Gazette*, *Guardian* 19 September 1986

Figure 24.3

Trends in wages

It appears that the UK's basic problem in terms of increases in its labour cost is now not one of slow growth of productivity but is due to relatively high wage settlements. Over the past three years UK earnings have continued to rise significantly more rapidly than in other countries. This is despite the fact that the UK inflation rate has fallen towards the average for the major six and despite the high level of unemployment which is still higher than most of the UK's major competitors.

The limited responsiveness of UK earnings to relatively low inflation and high unemployment is difficult to account for. A number of factors have been suggested in an attempt to explain it. One factor may be an increase in the structural mismatch between those skills most in demand and those of the unemployed. This mismatch may have resulted in upward pressure on some wage settlements. Another factor appears to be the growing segmentation in the labour market between those with jobs and those without. Much of the rise in unemployment in recent years has been associated with an increase in the duration of unemployment, and it is argued that the long-term unemployed are likely to have a diminishing effect over time on the wages of those in employment.

Recent figures indicate that wage rises are now showing a tendency to accelerate. The increase in average earnings which has been growing at a steady annual rate of 7.5 per cent since 1982, rose to 7.75 per cent in November and December 1986. Conditions therefore appear set for a steady rise in wage settlements and continued buoyancy in earnings. This situation has precipitated calls, from the Employment Minister as noted above, for the end to national pay bargaining, also the abolition of the annual pay round and pay determined as near as possible to the shop floor. These changes are necessary, it is argued, in order to allow a widening of regional pay differentials, which should then raise the demand for labour in the areas where unemployment is greatest. But the CBI has pointed out that national pay deals help to minimize the 'leap frogging' which generates wage inflation. Also, national agreements set minimum wage rates and substantial regional variations already exist. Although a further widening of regional wage differentials may encourage employers to hire more workers in high unemployment areas the effect might be countered by the reduction in local purchasing power as relative wages fell. Some observers argue that a better solution would be to cut employers' National Insurance contributions in the high unemployment areas, as this would avoid the problem of the loss in local purchasing power and would be a speedier solution than a campaign to decentralize pay bargaining.

Source: *British Economy Survey* Spring, 1987

Figure 24.1
There is a difference between wages, earnings, and total rewards for work. Comparisons are frequently made between the wages paid to different groups of workers. These comparisons may be misleading because employers do not only reward their workers through basic pay. Workers may receive additional remuneration in the form of overtime and bonuses. They may also receive fringe benefits that do not appear as part of earnings. Generally speaking, the higher the level of earnings of an employee in the UK, the more valuable will be their fringe benefits: this is not necessarily the case in other industrialized nations.

1. What is the difference between (**a**) wages, (**b**) earnings, and (**c**) total rewards for employment?
2. What fringe benefits might be available to (**a**) a company director, and (**b**) a nurse?

Figure 24.2
A distinction needs to be made between real and money earnings. Since the end of the Second World War in 1945 the average price level has risen every year, and since 1970 the level of inflation has rarely been below 5 per cent. This means that workers have required a wage rise each year equal to or above the rate of inflation to maintain their real wages. It is important to realize that the purchasing power of wages depends on the extent to which wages can keep ahead of the rate of inflation.

3. Name one period in which the purchasing power of earnings actually fell.
4. What was happening to living standards of the average person in paid work from 1982? Explain your answer.

Figure 24.3
There is rarely a single explanation for economic events. Sometimes newspapers and magazine articles will claim a simple explanation for a particular economic event. Only on rare occasions will apparently simple explanations be accepted by economists as sufficient: an example is the claim that inflation is always and only caused by an increase in the supply of money. Most economists would accept that economic events happen for a variety of reasons which may be interconnected in a complex manner.

5. What economic phenomenon puzzled economists in the 1980s because theoretically it should not have occurred?

APPLYING ECONOMIC PRINCIPLES

1. (**a**) How can some of the earnings differentials in Figure 24.1 be explained by economic theory? Use diagrams in your answer. (**b**) What economic arguments can be made (**i**) for (**ii**) against paying a company chairman or managing director over one hundred and thirty times more than a nurse? the 1980s have been giving concern to the government? (**e**) With reference to productivity, under what circumstances would a government *not* be concerned about a rise in real wages?

2. With reference to Figure 24.2: (**a**) Describe the trends shown, referring to real and money wages in your answer. With reference to Figure 24.2 and 24.3: (**b**) (**i**) What did economists expect to happen to real earnings in the early 1980s when inflation reached 20 per cent per annum and unemployment reached 3¼ million? Give reasons for their expectations. (**ii**) What actually did happen to real wages in this period? (**iii**) Give two possible reasons why real earnings did not respond as expected, explaining the terms 'structural mismatch' and 'growing segmentation in the labour market' in your answer. (**c**) Explain how the NAIRU (sometimes known as the natural rate of unemployment) theory could be used to explain the simultaneous existence of high unemployment and a high rate of real wage increases. (**d**) For what reasons might the growth in real wages towards the end of

3. With reference to Figure 24.3: (**a**) Explain the meaning of the phrase 'a widening of regional pay differentials'. (**b**) (**i**) What two features of pay bargaining in the UK did the Employment Minister wish to see abolished to allow for a widening of regional pay differentials? (**ii**) Draw a supply and demand diagram for the labour market to show how a national wage rate set above the market wage rate could affect the market for labour. (**c**) (**i**) Explain how shop floor pay bargaining could help the labour market to clear. (**ii**) Explain how structural mismatch and growing segmentation of the labour market could prevent the market clearing even with shop floor pay bargaining. (**d**) What economic arguments might be put forward against the abolition of national wage bargaining and the introduction of shop floor wage bargaining?

FOR FURTHER INVESTIGATION
Collect some job advertisements from local and national newspapers. List the jobs and the rates of pay being offered. Note down any fringe benefits, and try to make an estimate of their monetary worth. Draw a bar chart to record your findings. Divide the bar up into actual pay, and pay plus the estimated value of fringe benefits. Use economic analysis to write an account of your findings.

ESSAYS
Refer to the data wherever possible, especially in the first essay.
1. (**a**) What type of employees tends to earn the highest salaries in the UK, and why? (**b**) Under what circumstances might employees willingly accept a fall in their nominal wage increases year after year? Explain your answer.
2. To what extent can minimum wage legislation solve the problem of low pay? [London 6/87]

Making the most of it

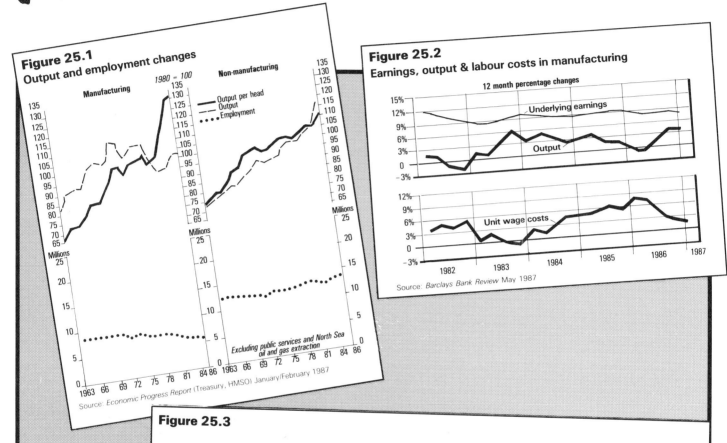

Figure 25.1
Output and employment changes

Source: *Economic Progress Report* (Treasury, HMSO) January/February 1987

Figure 25.2
Earnings, output & labour costs in manufacturing

Source: *Barclays Bank Review* May 1987

Figure 25.3

Productivity and unemployment

Many people fear that measures which increase productivity will mean that the same output is produced by a smaller labour force, thus raising unemployment. This obviously does not apply to improvements in average productivity brought about by the introduction of new products or the development of new industries. But it is easy to see how such a fear arises when production is concentrated in more efficient units or new labour-saving equipment is installed; for if we consider a single plant or firm it is true that, unless sales are increased, higher productivity does mean fewer jobs. However, it does not necessarily follow that jobs are lost in the economy as a whole. Only if the *aggregate* demand for goods and services of all kinds in the economy was constant, or did not increase by enough to absorb the labour released when productivity rises, would this be the case.

Fortunately, rising productivity in the economy can be expected to create a demand for the extra output which an unchanged labour force can produce. Someone must benefit from the increase in productivity—the worker in the form of higher real wages, the employer in the form of higher profits or reduced losses, or the customer in the form of lower prices. Normally there will in fact be an element of each of these, the division depending on the nature and strength of competition in the markets for the goods or services produced and in the labour market. But whatever the division, there are reasons why aggregate demand should rise.

To see why, we need to trace the impact of each of these through the economic system. To the extent that the workforce receives higher real wages it will spend more on consumption, and firms which earn higher profits will invest more or pay higher dividends. If prices are held down

customers' real incomes will be increased, enabling them to increase their purchases of goods and services generally. Of course part of the higher real incomes may be saved, part will certainly be paid in taxes, and part will be spent on imports or, through a lower price of exports, benefit the customer abroad. However, higher savings should feed back into demand through the workings of the capital market (or the foreign exchange market if the savings are lent abroad)—interest rates should be lower or credit more readily available; the additional tax receipts would allow the government to cut tax rates or increase expenditure without any rise in the public sector borrowing requirement—something which could be expected to occur if the government correctly interpreted the rates of productivity growth; and the exchange rate should adjust to avoid any permanent leakage of demand abroad.

Source: *Midland Bank Review* Winter 1984

Figure 25.1
The choice of scales on a line graph can affect the visual impact of a trend. Axes may be carefully chosen to increase or reduce the impact of a set of statistics presented graphically. For example, critics of the government might use axes in such a way as to show a very steep rise in unemployment: the government may change the axes so that the rise looks less dramatic. When studying graphs it is always worth considering who produced the graph, and especially whether they tend to support government policy or not.

1. (a) For what reasons might the scale of employment graphs go up to 25 million even though employment is never higher than 15 million? (b) (i) Sketch the employment graph for manufacturing between 1963 and 1986 using one centimetre for 1 million employees, and two centimetres for every five years. (ii) What is the main difference in the visual impact of your graph and the one in Figure 25.1?

2. Consider the source of this graph and give a possible reason why the graph of employment in manufacturing has been presented in the way that it has.

Figure 25.2
A fall in the rate of increase should not be confused with an absolute fall. When a line graph falls it must be studied carefully to see whether it shows an absolute fall in a variable, or just a fall in the rate of increase in the variable. For example, a graph showing falling inflation would still be showing rising prices: it would be the rate at which prices are rising which would have fallen.

3. In which periods did output fall?
4. In which period(s) did the percentage increase in earnings increase?

Figure 25.3
It is important to identify the progression of analysis in documentary data. Economic analysis frequently follows through logically the consequences of an economic change on the economy. The effect of an economic change is analogous to throwing a pebble in a pool: the ripples affect the pool over a wide area. In a similar way an economic change, such as a tax cut, will have significant primary effects on the immediate recipients, and secondary multiplier effects throughout the rest of the economy. Such changes can often be usefully summarized in a flow chart or similar diagram.

5. Draw a flow chart showing the effects of increasing productivity on the economy.

APPLYING ECONOMIC PRINCIPLES

1. With reference to Figure 25.1: (a) Explain the difference between output and productivity. (b) Describe the relationship between output and productivity between 1963 and 1979. (c) Give reasons for this relationship. (d) (i) What was unusual about the relationship between 1980 and 1982 in manufacturing? (ii) With reference to employment in manufacturing over the same period, give a reason for the unusual relationship. (e) Describe and explain the differences in the trends in manufacturing and non-manufacturing productivity after 1979.

2. With reference to Figure 25.2: (a) Describe and explain the relationship between output, earnings and unit labour costs. (b) What would be the effect on unit labour costs of a sharp increase in earnings with output and employment unchanged? Explain your answer.

3. (a) Use supply and demand diagrams to show the effects of a rise in productivity in a given industry on (i) the labour market, and (ii) the goods market. (b) What factors could cause an increase in productivity? (c) Why do the effects shown in (a) suggest that increases in productivity can lead to a higher standard of living for the workforce? (d) How can productivity and investment be related in a 'virtuous circle'?

4. Refer to Figure 25.3. (a) How can a rise in productivity be associated with (i) a fall in employment in an industry, and (ii) a rise in employment in the whole economy? (b) (i) Which three withdrawals from the circular flow of income are referred to in the last paragraph? (ii) Although a rise in productivity may increase these withdrawals in the short term, how does the article suggest that, despite these withdrawals, national income may still increase in the long run?

5. Assess the costs and benefits of an increase in productivity achieved by the introduction of new machinery in a particular industry (i) in the short-term, and (ii) in the long-term for: (a) workers in the industry; (b) consumers of the industry's products.

FOR FURTHER INVESTIGATION
Many people believe that the UK has a very poor productivity record relative to other developed nations. Try to find some figures which will provide evidence for, or refute, this view. Produce your evidence in a report and suggest reasons for the UK's record. Suggest measures that the government could take to improve productivity in the UK.

ESSAYS
Refer to the data wherever possible, especially in the first essay.
1. (a) Describe and account for the changes in unit labour costs in the UK in the 1980s. (b) Why might it be considered important for an economy that unit labour costs fall?
2. 'Britain is a low productivity, low wage economy. West Germany is a high productivity, high wage economy.' Discuss. [Cambridge 12/83]

Advancing years

Figure 26.1
The population of the UK by age

(000's)	1901	1951	1986
Under 5	4 831	4 325	3 642
5–14	8 040	6 999	7 157
15–64	23 557	33 433	37 281
65–74	1 278	3 689	5 005
75–84	470	1 555	2 969
85†	61	224	709
Total UK population	**38 237**	**50 225**	**56 763**

Source: *Annual Abstract of Statistics*

Figure 26.2
Average life expectancy at birth

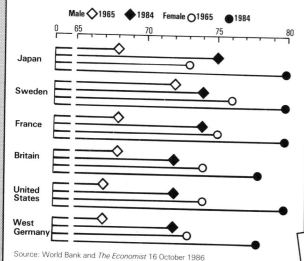

Source: World Bank and *The Economist* 16 October 1986

Figure 26.3

Grey power

Social Trends, the government's annual orgy of number-crunching on population and other demographic trends, spells it out: In 1985, there were some 9.3 million people in the 45–59 age group — by 2015, 28 years away, the government predicts a rise to 12.6 million. In the 60–74 age group, the comparable rise is from 8 million to 9.1 million.

In comparison, the 15–29 segment, so beloved of the fashion, drink and leisure companies, is declining. Having grown steadily over the past 35 years—10.2 million in 1951, 13.4 million in 1985, *Social Trends* predicts that this category will slump to 10.8 million in 2001, picking up to 12 million in 2015.

It isn't that the population is growing dramatically as a whole — it has hovered between 55.9 million and 56.6 million since 1971 and the government doesn't expect it to top 59.6 million by 2015 — but the age structure within the population has changed radically.

While the percentage of 60s and over was less than eight in 1901, by 1985 this group represented 20 per cent of the total population. In numerical terms, the figure rose by around 2.5 million between 1961 and 1985, and is expected to increase by another 2 million by 2015. Similarly, the under 15s, who represented 19 per cent of the total population in 1985, will form just 18 per cent of the 2015 UK population

Source: *Guardian* 23 April 1987

Figure 26.4

BMA issues warning on old age

The number of people over 85 will rise by 54 per cent in the next 20 years, threatening a "health care catastrophe," the British Medical Association said yesterday.

It adds: "The general treatment of the frail elderly by the state is a scandal. Lack of money and bureaucratic confusion has left a legacy from the Victorian era with the state looking backwards, remodelling ancient buildings and patching up a system of care which is fragmentary, pitifully inadequate and increasingly inadequate to the elderly age group."

The report welcomes, provided that there are safeguards, the boom in private sheltered housing and the development of alarm call systems to help the better off elderly. But it says this must be balanced by more investment in rented local authority and housing association accommodation for the poorest.

The doctors want better hospital facilities for the elderly, better training for consultants helping the elderly, and more support for the carers of the elderly.

Source: *All Our Tomorrows* (BMA; 1987) and *Guardian* 13 March 1986

Figure 26.5

The outnumbered generation

In 1980, there were 6.3 million teenagers; in 1994, there will be 4.6 millions. Thus the drop over the decade will be slightly over 25 per cent. In the same period, the number of young adults between 20 and 24 will fall by 900,000 to 3.9 millions — a reduction of 18 per cent. There will be a mini baby boom, it is forecast, so from 1995, the UK population — virtually stable for a decade — will go up very slightly.

There will be important, consequences for governments, in their economic and social policies; to employers, and to the leisure and service industries particularly. So far, there are few signs that central government departments are taking account of the population shift. The exception is education: the fall in numbers is now affecting sixth forms. Typical is the situation in Bath, where the debate centred on which of the city's five secondary schools should lose their sixth forms. The compromise reached was to combine all the A level intake in one sixth-form college.

Thus, at a simple level, a drop in numbers of teenagers means an over-provision of services.

There are going to be similar decisions to be faced in other social policy fields: if there are fewer teenagers committing fewer crimes (this correlation does not necessarily follow, of course) there will be fewer probation officers, social workers and community homes needed for them. Half the abortions in Britain involve women between 16 and 24; will we need fewer facilities for terminations; fewer intensive care units for teenagers involved in serious car and motorbike accidents? Fewer places on Youth Training Programmes?

Source: *Guardian* 29 September 1985

Figure 26.1
Changing the presentation of data may help to clarify trends.
Statistics can be presented in a variety of ways. Different methods of presentation will have different advantages and disadvantages. A table of figures may be the best method of presenting fairly precise information where exact figures are required. Pie charts, bar charts and line graphs might be preferable to highlight a pattern or trend.

1. Represent Figure 26.1 as a series of bar charts showing the percentage of the population in each age group in the three years.

2. What advantage has this method of presentation over the table?

Figure 26.2
Some variables are difficult to measure and other data may be used to indicate changes in them. It is not always possible to define and measure variables precisely in economics. The level of demand, for example, is not directly measured, but other indicators such as the level of unemployment and value of retail sales are used to estimate the level of demand.

3. What economic variable is average life expectancy sometimes used to help measure?

4. What problems could arise when using life expectancy in this way?

Figure 26.3
Changing the presentation of data may help to clarify trends. The point made for Figure 26.1 about statistical data would also apply to documentary data. Articles frequently contain a great deal of statistical material which may conveniently be arranged in another form for the purpose of analysis.

5. Present as much of the data as possible in Figure 26.3 in tabular form.

Figure 26.4
Emotive words may be used to give emphasis to an economic change. Writers often feel very strongly about the subject on which they are writing, and the language they use might reflect this. For example, words like 'crash' and 'meltdown' were used to describe the sharp fall in share prices in October 1987.

6. List three words or phrases in the passage which are used to elicit an emotional response in the reader.

Figure 26.5
It is important to identify the progression of analysis in documentary data. Economic analysis frequently follows through logically the consequences of an economic change on the economy. A flow chart or similar method of presentation can help to clarify the process of logical deduduction which is taking place.

7. Draw a flow chart to show the effects that the change in population indicated here will have on government provision of services.

APPLYING ECONOMIC PRINCIPLES

1. With reference to Figure 26.1: (a) Explain, using figures, the link between trends in the under-5 population and trends in the 75+ population in later years. (b) (i) What predictions could you make about the age structure of the population in 2005 from the data? Explain your answer. (ii) What changes could occur that would explain a difference between your predicted change, and what actually happens?

2. With reference to Figure 26.3 and 26.5: (a) Draw demand and supply curves to show the effect of the changes in age distribution predicted on: (i) the market for an arthritis drug, (ii) the market for pop records. (b) (i) What is likely to happen to the demand for fashion clothing in future years? Give reasons for your answer. (ii) How might this affect costs of production and competition for mass producers and for small specialist retailers? (iii) Besides population structure changes, what other factors will affect the demand for fashion clothing in the longer-term?

3. Refer to Figure 26.4: (a) What recommendations does the report make to policy makers to take account of demographic changes over the next 20 years? (b) Explain at least three possible ways in which the finance needed for these schemes may be obtained, and analyse the possible economic effects of each option.

4. Refer to Figure 26.2: (a) What do the data suggest about (i) relative standards of living, and (ii) changes in the standards of living in the countries shown? Explain your answers. (b) What other information would you need to investigate the average standard of living of a country's citizens?

5. (a) Given a choice, should the government spend more on building homes for very old people, or should it provide more financial help and more social workers to help relatives look after elderly people at home? Give reasons for your answer. (b) What are the external costs of the government failing to provide adequately for the increase in the number of very old people?

FOR FURTHER INVESTIGATION
Using statistical data for your local region or area, find out what changes there have been in recent years to the population structure. Write a report analysing these changes, using statistical information to support your presentation. The report should contain a written account of the changes, and what you consider to be the implications for future planning in the social services, leisure and educational fields.

As well as obtaining data from books and other written sources, you may also consider interviewing some retired people to see what they consider to be their needs and wants, and to what extent these are being met by private and public sectors.

ESSAYS
Refer to the data wherever possible, especially in the first essay.

1. (a) What have been the major changes in the age distribution of the UK population in recent years? (b) What are the reasons for the changes? (c) What effect will a reduction in the number of teenagers have on unemployment? Explain your answer.

2. Discuss the economic consequences of an ageing population. [London 1/87]

Jobs for the girls

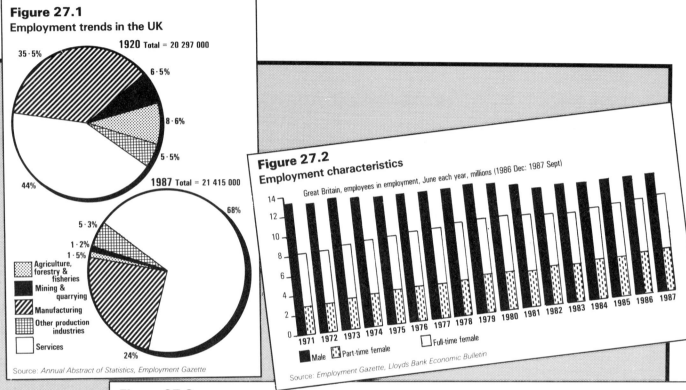

Figure 27.1
Employment trends in the UK

1920 Total = 20 297 000

35·5%
6·5%
8·6%
5·5%
44%

1987 Total = 21 415 000

68%
5·3%
1·2%
1·5%
24%

Agriculture, forestry & fisheries
Mining & quarrying
Manufacturing
Other production industries
Services

Source: *Annual Abstract of Statistics, Employment Gazette*

Figure 27.2
Employment characteristics

Great Britain, employees in employment, June each year, millions (1986 Dec: 1987 Sept)

1971 1972 1973 1974 1975 1976 1977 1978 1979 1980 1981 1982 1983 1984 1985 1986 1987

Male Part-time female Full-time female

Source: *Employment Gazette, Lloyds Bank Economic Bulletin*

Figure 27.3

The phenomenon of part-time employment in Britain

IN NON-MANUFACTURING industries employers have for several years been using part-time labour in the course of expanding the provision of services to include weekend and late evening operations, whilst reducing the working week of full-time employees to five days. Levels of part-time employment in the female labour force range from 12 per cent in transport catering to over 80 per cent amongst clerical staff in credit card banking, and to more than 90 per cent in manual occupations in local authorities, hospitals, pubs and clubs. Part-time labour is used more flexibly than in manufacturing establishments to meet fluctuations in daily and weekly trading. In branch banking part-time clerks are employed by the day or half-day each week, on alternate weeks, and for month end and other seasonal duties. Sales assistants in retail distribution work on Saturday only, on Saturdays and Mondays, and at peak trading times throughout a six-day week. Those who work on Saturdays only are employed for $7\frac{1}{2}$ hours, those working for two days for $15\frac{1}{2}$ hours, with almost 30 per cent at particular stores working for fewer than

8 hours per week, and some 20 per cent for fewer than 16 hours. By replacing one full-time sales assistant with two or three part-timers, employers can save as much as 8 manhours per week. It is deployment of labour in this manner that accounts for the decrease from 21.6 to 18.9 hours in the average basic part-time working week in retailing since 1975, an industry where the proportion of female sales assistants working part-time has risen from 50 to 60 per cent.

In local authority education departments at least 10 per cent of clerical workers have weekly hours of fewer than 16, and 50 per cent of the part-timers engaged to work during term time only, in the lowest graded non-manual occupation of ancillary assistant, work for no more than 16 hours per week. The school meals service is staffed predominantly by women on weekly contracts of $5\frac{1}{2}$ to $12\frac{1}{2}$ hours, and some 80 per cent of school cleaners are employed for under 21 hours per week. In hospitals all domestic assistants employed on similar contracts are female part-timers. Part-time nurses nonetheless, tend generally to be engaged for

longer hours, on regular night or weekend work, with increasing numbers of both qualified and auxiliary nurses working from 16 to 21 hours, enabling management to cope with the reduction from 40 to $37\frac{1}{2}$ hours in the full-time nurses' working week implemented in 1980–81.

In the hotel and catering trades where two-thirds of the labour force are female and of whom 73 per cent are part-time, the long-term downward trend in part-time hours is widely reflected. Although in much of the industry part-time employment is regarded as work of fewer than 39 hours per week, 25 to 35 per cent of women in the principal occupations of counterhands and kitchenhands work for fewer than 16 hours, and a further 25 per cent for 16 to 21 hours. Weekly hours of fewer than 16 are worked by catering staff at airports, motorway service stations, railways and hospitals, at times not adequately covered by the schedules of full-time workers employed on rotating shift systems geared to 24 hour and seven-day service.

Source: Olive Robinson, *National Westminster Bank Review* November 1985

Figure 27.1
Data on employment may use a variety of ways of classifying industries. Economists often classify industries as either 'primary', 'secondary' or 'tertiary' for the purpose of analysing employment changes. These categories do not appear in government statistics: in many official government publications employment is divided into 'agriculture, forestry and fishing', 'production industries', 'construction industries', and 'services'. Variations on these categories will appear in other statistical sources.

1. Which two categories shown on the pie chart would economists classify as 'primary industries'?

2. To what extent does the right-hand pie chart suggest that a new classification of industries might be required in future?

Figure 27.2
Data may contain information on both "patterns" and "trends". A 'pattern' refers to a distribution at a particular time. For example, the pattern of employment in the UK would refer to the number of workers in different types of jobs in the current year. Statistics may also be used to find trends: a trend would refer to the change in a pattern over a period of time. For example, the trend in employment in the UK would refer to how the types of jobs that workers are doing are changing over a period of time.

3. Describe the pattern of employment shown for Great Britain in 1987.

4. Describe, using figures, the most significant trends shown in the data.

Figure 27.3
It is important to distinguish the main points in articles that provide a large number of examples. It is easy to forget, or to fail to recognize, the main point of an article, where a large amount of statistical data is given or a large number of examples are presented. Long articles need to be read carefully to discover the point or points that the examples are designed to illustrate.

5. What is the main point of this article?

APPLYING ECONOMIC PRINCIPLES

1. With reference to Figure 27.1: **(a)** Describe the trends shown in the pie charts. **(b)** Explain the major reasons for the trends. **(c)** Which of reasons for job losses in manufacturing could account for job losses in some of the service industries in future years? Give examples. **(d)** For what reasons might increases in service sector employment fail to reduce unemployment significantly among redundant workers in secondary industries?

2. With reference to Figure 27.3: **(a)** Give examples of occupations where by 1985 the incidence of part-time work was very high in the UK. **(b)** Why has part-time employment been increasing in recent years? **(c)** What are the economic implications of an increase in part-time employment?

3. The number of employees in service jobs is much higher than the figures shown in Figure 27.1. Only one fifth of workers in a large firm making telephone systems were found to be 'manufacturing' whilst the rest, though officially classified as manufacturing workers, were in service jobs. **(a)** List three service industry-type jobs that might be carried out by workers in a large car factory. **(b)** Explain the effect of continuing technological change on employment patterns in the motor industry.

4. The changing nature of employment, leading to an increase in female part-time, unskilled, non-unionised employment, has affected the supply of labour and its elasticity. **(a)** Draw a supply and demand diagram for an industry increasing its use of this type of labour and decreasing full-time male employment. Show the demand curve for labour, and the supply curve before and after the change. Show the effect on wage rates and employment levels in the industry. Explain fully the effects identified. **(b)** In what circumstances could the effects shown in **(a)**: **(i)** reduce aggregate demand, and **(ii)** increase aggregate demand?

5. (a) Draw labour market supply and demand diagrams to show the theoretical effect on the decline in employment in manufacturing industries based in the North, and the expansion of service industries based in the South. You should draw separate diagrams for each of these labour markets to show the effects on employment and wage rates in each market. **(b)** Explain how this process should theoretically create full employment equilibrium in the economy. **(c) (i)** What rigidities in labour markets might prevent this process from occurring? **(ii)** What policies could be used to overcome such rigidities?

FOR FURTHER INVESTIGATION
There have been major changes not only between employment sectors, but also within employment sectors. The *Annual Abstract of Statistics* available at all main reference libraries, contains a detailed breakdown of the number of workers within each main employment sector. Write a report analysing the changes within the manufacturing sector of the economy, describing which industries have declined most in employment. Suggest reasons for the trends that you have discovered. Use tables, bar charts and other methods of statistical presentation to support your analysis.

ESSAYS
Refer to the data wherever possible, especially in the first essay.

1. For what reasons might the employment prospects for a middle-aged unemployed male steelworker be so poor in modern Britain?

2. Give examples of low paid workers in Britain and suggest reasons why they are low paid. Would a national minimum wage improve the position of the low paid in Britain? [JMB 6/85]

North and South

Figure 28.1
GDP per head and employment changes

	Gross Domestic Product per head (UK = 100)		Employment: % change
	1975	1984	1979–86
South East	113	117	+2
East Midlands	96	99	nil
East Anglia	93	98	+13
Scotland	98	96	−8
North West	96	96	−12
South West	90	95	+5
West Midlands	100	90	−7
North	94	90	−10
Yorkshire and Humberside	94	88	−6
Wales	88	86	−13
Northern Ireland	80	78	n.a

Source: Financial Times and British Economy Survey Spring 1987

Figure 28.2
The growing North-South divide

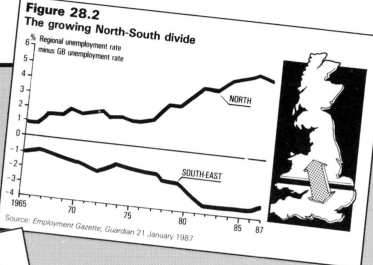

Source: Employment Gazette, Guardian 21 January 1987

Figure 28.3
Ranking of counties by relative concentrations of high tech

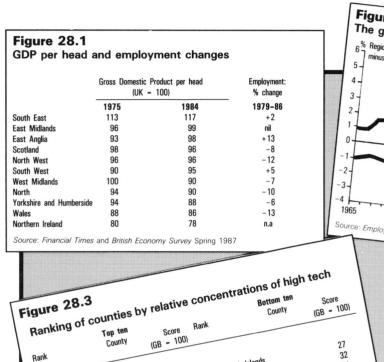

Rank	Top ten County	Score (GB = 100)	Rank	Bottom ten County	Score (GB = 100)
1.	Hertforshire	224	1.	Scottish Islands	27
2.	Berkshire	195	2.	Powys	32
3.	Gloucestershire	171	3.	South Yorkshire	34
4.	Surrey	168	4.	Dyfed	34
5.	Hampshire	158	5.	Shropshire	37
6.	West Sussex	155	6.	West Glamorgan	39
7.	Avon	155	7.	Lincolnshire	42
8.	Isle of Wight	153	8.	Grampian	42
9.	Dorset	146	9.	North Yorkshire	44
10.	Somerset	139	10.	Central Scotland	45

Note: scores are computed by measuring the proportion of high tech in total employment in each county: and comparing the county score with the average for Great Britain.

Source: Guardian 3 June 1987

Figure 28.4

The North-South problem

In recent years the whole question of regional disparities in the British economy has often been abbreviated into the politically contentious form of the 'North/South' problem. The trends in employment and level of income in Wales and East Anglia, for example, almost suggest that it is just as much a 'West/East' problem. What is indisputable is that major disparities in economic performance between the principal regions of Britain remain, even after more than fifty years of policies by many different governments to deal with them. The most important statistical facts concern employment, income *per capita*, growth rates, and social amenities, especially housing.

Disparities as great as these clearly create social and economic problems and in themselves may be considered unjust. Regions of low income and high unemployment tend to lose younger and more enterprising people to the better-off regions; social capital deteriorates; new firms are reluctant to find sites; house prices fall relatively. The problem is cumulative, as the statistics indicate with their wider disparities in the 1980s. Successive governments have fought a losing battle with these trends, usually by demarcating various types of areas which have been given preferential treatment for tax purposes, in planning controls and with the provision of capital.

Source: British Economy Survey Spring 1987

Figure 28.1
A rise or fall in an index number does not necessarily indicate a rise or fall in an absolute value. Index numbers are very useful for showing percentage changes; however, they do not necessarily show whether a particular value has increased or decreased. For example, index numbers could be used to compare regional house prices with the national average. If the index number for house prices in (say) the North fell, it would probably indicate that house prices were rising less quickly in the North than in the country as a whole: it would probably not mean that house prices were actually falling in the North.

1. Can you infer that GDP per head in the West Midlands was lower in 1984 than in 1975? Explain your answer.

2. Can you infer that the unemployment rate was lower in the South East in 1986 than in 1979? Explain your answer.

Figure 28.2
The country may be divided into regions for the purpose of economic analysis, but there may be significant variations within regions. For the purpose of economic analysis the country may be divided into different parts. Figure 28.1 shows the standard planning regions that appear in many official statistics. Whatever divisions are used, they will still mask considerable variations within regions. For example, house prices in the North may be on average significantly below those in the South, but in some areas in the North house prices may be very high compared to the region as a whole.

3. By referring to Figure 28.1, explain why the simple North-South divide on the map here (Figure 28.2) is somewhat misleading.

4. Explain how the map is inconsistent with the line graph which it accompanies.

Figure 28.3
The correct meaning of numerical values must be identified. Many figures that appear in statistics will be easily understood because they occur frequently. Some figures are unusual and require careful interpretation. Often, unusual statistics — for example, the location quotient used here — will be explained in a footnote.

5. Does the figure of 244 for Hertfordshire mean that: (a) There are 244,000 high tech workers in Hertfordshire. (b) Hertfordshire has about 24.4 per cent of the high tech workers in GB. (c) The proportion of workers in high tech in Hertfordshire is about 2½ times the national average. (d) Herfordshire has almost ten times the number of high tech workers as the Scottish Islands?

6. What does the figure of 45 for Central Scotland mean?

Figure 28.4
It is important to distinguish social problems and economic problems whilst recognizing their interdependence. Some economic problems have great adverse consequences for the lives of ordinary people. For example, high unemployment may be a contributory factor in social problems such as inner city riots, marital breakdown and suicide, as well as creating economic problems such as wasted resources and decaying infrastructure. It is important to recognize the connection between economic problems and the social problems that might arise as a result of them.

7. Describe (a) two social problems, and (b) two economic problems that could be caused by the migration referred to in the article.

APPLYING ECONOMIC PRINCIPLES

1. (a) Many economists suggest that there is a North-South divide if the dividing line is taken from the Severn to the Wash. With reference to Figures 28.1 and 28.3 what evidence is there to suggest that this hypothesis is correct? Refer to Figure 28.4. (b) What is meant by 'regional disparities'? (c) Give three measures of regional disparities. (d) (i) Describe how regional disparities affect internal migration within the UK (ii) How might this create a vicious circle of decline in some areas?

2. (a) Why do regional disparities occur? (b) (i) With reference to Figure 28.4, what has the government attempted to do about regional disparities? (ii) With reference to Figures 28.2 and 28.4, what degree of success have they had? (iii) In view of the government's record, should they spend more or less on regional policy in future? Explain your answer.

3. It is argued by some economists that regional disparities would largely disappear if wages fell low enough in depressed regions. (a) Why might lower wages help to reduce regional differences? (b) Give possible reasons why wages may fail to fall to the level needed to eliminate unemployment in depressed regions. (c) Draw a supply and demand diagram for workers in a declining industry to show how a fall in demand for their services leads to a lower market wage for them. (d) Draw a supply and demand diagram to show how the labour market in the South East might be affected by economic expansion. (e) Why might high regional unemployment persist even if wages in depressed and prosperous regions adjust as predicted in neo-classical theory?

4. (a) Give possible reasons for the regional pattern of advanced technology identified in Figure 28.3. (b) With reference to Figure 28.3, and your answer to (a), explain how the South can benefit from external economies in advanced technology.

5. What external costs are associated with regional disparities: (a) for a region dominated by a declining industry? (b) for the South East?

FOR FURTHER INVESTIGATION
Using statistical data for your local region or area, compare the economic position of the region or area with the UK as a whole. Figure 28.4 gives at least four different measures that could be used for comparison, e.g. gross domestic product per capita. Use the information to write a report analysing the economic differences between your region and the UK as a whole. Include bar charts, tables, etc to support your answer. Explain any variation between your region and the nation as a whole.

ESSAYS
Refer to the data wherever possible, especially in the first essay.

1. (a) What evidence is there to suggest that regional disparities in the UK are increasing? (b) For what reasons might they go on increasing?

2. Outline the influences which are chiefly responsible for the pattern of urban and regional unemployment in Britain. Does economics give any guidance as to whether or not it is desirable or possible to do anything to change this pattern? [JMB 6/85]

Rags and riches

Figure 29.1
Percentage shares of income, before and after tax, received by quantile groups (UK)

Quantile group		Before tax[2] 1978/79	1981/82	1984/85	After tax[2] 1978/79	1981/82	1984/85
Top 1	per cent	5.3	6.0	6.4	3.9	4.6	4.9
2–5	per cent	10.7	11.6	12.1	9.8	10.7	11.1
6–10	per cent	10.1	10.7	10.9	9.7	10.3	10.5
Top 10	per cent	26.1	28.3	29.5	23.4	25.6	26.5
11–20	per cent	16.5	16.7	16.8	16.3	16.4	16.6
21–30	per cent	13.5	13.2	13.0	13.5	13.2	13.0
31–40	per cent	11.2	10.7	10.3	11.3	10.8	10.4
41–50	per cent	9.2	8.6	8.2	9.3	8.8	8.6
51–60	per cent	7.3	7.0	6.6	7.7	7.3	7.1
61–70	per cent	5.8	5.8	5.4	6.4	6.3	6.0
71–80	per cent	4.5	4.4	4.4	5.1	5.2	4.9
81–90	per cent	3.5	3.5	3.5	4.1	4.0	4.2
91–100	per cent	2.4	2.0	2.3	2.9	2.4	2.7
Median income: £		3 370	4 720	5 480	2 890	4 090	4 990
Mean income: £		4 110	6 050	7 520	3 420	5 020	6 340
Gini: per cent		37	40	41	34	36	36

[1] The figures in this table are rounded and may therefore not sum to 100.
[2] People in, say, the top ten per cent of the pre-tax income distribution will not all be the same as those in the top ten per cent of the post-tax income distribution. This arises from differences in tax liability between one year and another. Undue significance should not be attached to very small changes, as the figures are rounded estimates.

Source: *Economic Trends* November 1987

Figure 29.2
Average income and tax paid by quantile group (UK)

1981/82

Quantile group		Average income (£) Before tax	After tax	Aver tax paid £	As percentage of pre-tax income
Top 1	per cent	36 300	22 840	13 460	37
Next 9	per cent	14 980	11 640	3 340	22
Next 40	per cent	7 440	6 160	1 280	17
Lower 50	per cent	2 720	2 550	170	6
Bottom 20	per cent	1 640	1 630	10	1
All tax-units		6 050	5 020	1 030	17

1984/85

Quantile group		Average income (£) Before tax	After tax	Average tax paid £	As percentage of pre-tax income
Top 1	per cent	48 210	30 940	17 270	36
Next 9	per cent	19 270	15 220	4 050	21
Next 40	per cent	9 090	7 660	1 430	16
Lower 50	per cent	3 340	3 190	150	4
Bottom 20	per cent	2 200	2 200	0	0
All tax-units		7 520	6 340	1 180	16

Note: The figures in this table are rounded and may therefore apparently differ from the sum of their constituents.

Source: *Economic Trends* November 1987

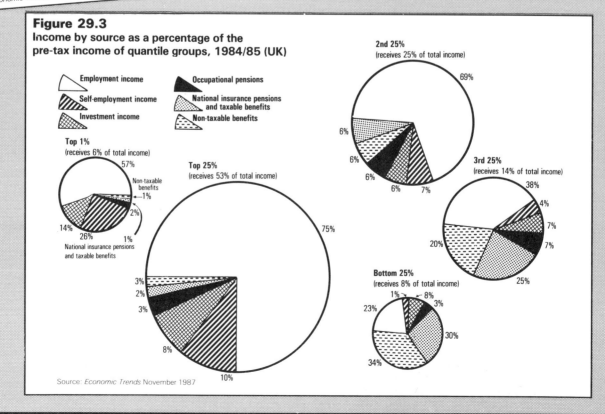

Figure 29.3
Income by source as a percentage of the pre-tax income of quantile groups, 1984/85 (UK)

Source: *Economic Trends* November 1987

Figure 29.1
The population may be divided into quantile groupings for the purpose of economic analysis. A study of the distribution of income and wealth involves looking at the differences between people according to how much income they earn or wealth they possess. In order to make comparisons the population may be divided up into quantile grouings, e.g. if the population were divided into deciles the income share of the top 10 per cent of income earners could be compared to the income of the next highest 10 per cent etc.

1. What percentage of total income was earned before tax by the top 5 per cent of income earners in (**a**) 1978/79, and (**b**) 1984/85?

2. What percentage of total income was earned before tax by the top 50 per cent of income earners in (**a**) 1978/79, and (**b**) 1984/85?

Figure 29.2
The use of averages can mask large variations within groups. Averages are used frequently in economics. For example, figures appear in the paper showing the national rate of unemployment or a regional average house price. However, a national unemployment rate of, say, 10 per cent may mask the fact that the unemployment rate in Northern Ireland may be over three times that of the South East of England.

3. What was the average income of the lowest 20 per cent of income earners, after tax, in (**a**) 1981/82, and (**b**) 1984/85?

4. Would you expect the deviation in income from the average to be greater for the top 1 per cent of income earners or the bottom 20 per cent of income earners? Explain your answer.

Figure 29.3
The term 'the distribution of income' can have different meanings in different contexts. The 'functional' distribution of income refers to the distribution of income according to which factor of production has earned the income, e.g. according to whether the income has been earned in the form of wages, rent, interest or profits. The distribution of income can also refer to the distribution between different quantile groups; and to the distribution according to source of income, e.g. wages, state benefits, pensions, etc.

5. What is the difference between the meaning of the distribution of income as shown here and as shown in Figures 29.1 and 29.2.

6. Approximately how much money did the top 1 per cent of income earners receive in investment income, before tax, in 1984/85? (You will need to refer also to Figure 29.2 to answer this question.)

APPLYING ECONOMIC PRINCIPLES

1. With reference to Figure 29.1: (**a**) Describe the pattern of income distribution, before tax, between the top 50 per cent of income earners and the bottom 50 per cent of income earners in 1978/79. (**b**) Describe the change in the pattern for the same quantile groups between 1978/79 and 1984/85. (**c**) What factors could explain the trend described in (**b**)?

2. Refer to Figure 29.2. (**a**) How much more did the highest 1 per cent of income earners earn on average than the lowest 20 per cent of income earners, before tax, in 1984/85? (**b**) What arguments could be put forward in favour of (**i**) reducing the differential, and (**ii**) increasing the differential?

3. (**a**) Refer to Figure 29.1. What effect did tax have on the percentage of income accounted for in 1984/85 by (**i**) the top 1 per cent of income earners, and (**ii**) the bottom 20 per cent of income earners? (**b**) Refer to Figure 29.2. What effect did tax have on the average income received in 1984/85 by (**i**) the top 1 per cent of income earners, and (**ii**) the bottom 20 per cent of income earners? (**c**) What do your answers to (**a**) and (**b**) tell you about the nature of the UK tax system? Explain your answer.

4. With reference to Figure 29.3: (**a**) Describe the pattern shown in the pie charts. (**b**) What possible reasons could explain the pattern shown? (**c**) What method of redistributing income is shown in the pie charts? Use figures to illustrate your answer.

5. (**a**) What is meant by 'the marginal propensity to consume'? (**b**) How is the redistribution of income by means of taxation and benefits, as shown in Figures 29.1 to 29.3, likely to affect the marginal propensity to consume? (**c**) With reference to macroeconomic policy objectives, what effects could result from a government policy which makes the distribution of income more equal? Use a diagram or diagrams to illustrate your answer.

FOR FURTHER INVESTIGATION
The Conservative Government elected in 1979, and re-elected in 1983 and 1987, believed that people in all income groups would benefit if income earners were allowed to keep a higher percentage of their income and pay less in taxation. They claimed that this would increase the incentive to work, and prevent a 'brain drain' of talent from the UK. Opponents of the Government argued that most people have not got the opportunity to work harder and, even if they have, tax cuts may reduce, rather than increase, the hours they choose to work.

Conduct a survey of people in work, preferably from different income groups. Try to find out whether the people have the opportunity to work more hours and/or work harder (e.g. by doing more overtime), and whether tax cuts would increase the quantity and/or quality of their work. Write a report stating whether, in the light of your survey, tax cuts can be justified in terms of increasing incentives to work.

ESSAYS
Refer to the data wherever possible, especially in the first essay.

1. (**a**) Was the UK Government in the 1980s successful in reducing the burden of income tax? (**b**) How are taxes and social security benefits used to redistribute income?

2. It has been suggested that the incentive to work in the UK will be increased by (**a**) a reduction in social security payments, and (**b**) a reduction in the higher rates of taxation. Explain and evaluate the reasoning underlying these views. [JMB 6/86]

Moving the goalposts

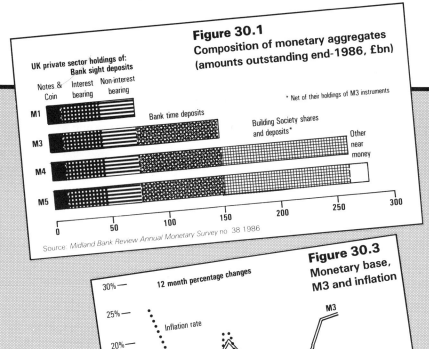

Figure 30.1
Composition of monetary aggregates
(amounts outstanding end-1986, £bn)

UK private sector holdings of:
Bank sight deposits

Notes & Coin | Interest bearing | Non-interest bearing

* Net of their holdings of M3 instruments

Bank time deposits

Building Society shares and deposits*

Other near money

M1 / M3 / M4 / M5

0   50   100   150   200   250   300

Source: *Midland Bank Review Annual Monetary Survey* no. 38 1986

Figure 30.2
Targets for M3 (formerly £M3)

Period of target	Target range	Out-turn
4/75– 4/77	9–13%	17.7%
4/77– 4/78	9–13%	16.0%
4/78– 4/79	8–12%	10.9%
10/78–10/79	8–12%	13.3%
6/79– 4/80	7–11%	10.3%
6/79–10/80	7–11%	17.8%
2/80–4/81	7–11%	18.5%
2/81–4/82	6–10%	14.5%
2/82–4/83	8–12%	11.0%
2/83–4/84	7–11%	9.7%
2/84–4/85	6–10%	12.2%
2/85–4/86	5–9%	16.6%
2/86–4/87	11–15%	19.0%

Source: *Bank of England Quarterly Bulletins*

Figure 30.3
Monetary base,
M3 and inflation

12 month percentage changes

30%
25%
20%
15%
10%
5%

Inflation rate

M3

M0

1975 '76 '77 '78 '79 '80 '81 '82 '83 '84 '85 '86 '87

Sources: Various

Figure 30.4
Counterparts of £M3

	(1) PSBR	(2) Net acquisition of public-sector debt by UK non-bank private sector	(3) Sterling leading to UK private sector	(4) Other counter parts (net)	(5) Increase in £M3
1980	11,813	9,425	10,025	–1818	10,595
1981	10,578	11,321	11,405	–1367	9,295
1982	4,953	10,618	17,556	–4368	7,523
1983	11,608	10,783	12,903	–4244	9,484
1984	10,239	11,155	16,541	–5855	9,860
1985	7,516	7,791	20,968	–5636	15,057
1986	2,502	4,052	29,367	–4567	23,250

Note: (5) = (1)–(2)+(3)+(4)   Counterparts to Changes in £M3 (£m)

Source: *Financial Statistics* 1987

Figure 30.5
Velocity of sterling M3[1]

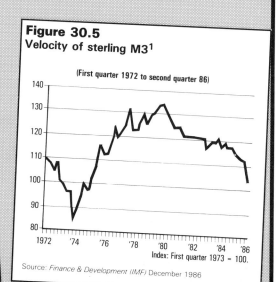

(First quarter 1972 to second quarter 86)

140
130
120
110
100
90
80

1972 '74 '76 '78 '80 '82 '84 '86

Index: First quarter 1973 = 100.

Source: *Finance & Development (IMF)* December 1986

Figure 30.1
Different measures of the money supply will appear in different data. There is no single definition of the money supply, and new measures are frequently introduced and other measures discarded. Newspapers and magazines may continue to refer to measures of the money supply which the government are no longer 'officially' using.

1. It can be inferred from the data that a particular measure of the money supply appears to have been discarded. Which measure?

Figure 30.2
It is important to recognize that government policies may be modified in the light of changing circumstances. A study of statistics can reveal that governments modify policy throughout their terms of office. For example, tax changes in a budget may reflect a change of government policy in respect of the redistribution of income.

2. The Medium-Term Financial Strategy (MTFS) introduced in 1979, aimed at a progressive reduction in the growth of M3. (a) On what occasions was this aim modified? (b) Do the data suggest a reason for its modification?

Figure 30.3
Official measures may be introduced or discarded to support economic theories and economic policies. The government publish statistics on a wide variety of matters. The choice of what to publish is not 'neutral': statistics may be carefully chosen for a particular reason. For example, the government introduced the Taxes and Prices Index because they were keen to show wage bargainers that if taxes had been cut they would not need wage rises in line with inflation to maintain their standard of living.

3. With reference to the data, explain why a government that believed in a close relationship between the money supply and inflation might officially target M0 as a measure of the money supply rather than M3.

Figure 30.4
Individuals, organizations and economies may be grouped for the purpose of analysis. Institutions are often classified, for example, under the headings 'public sector' and 'private sector' for the purpose of comparing different types of economy. Economies are often described as 'developed' or 'developing' for the purpose of analysing economic development.

4. What is meant by 'the non-bank private sector'?

Figure 30.5
Some statistics are calculated from other statistics and not measured in their own right. Some variables are difficult to measure in themselves, and they may be calculated from other figures. For example, the amount of saving in the economy tends to be estimated by deducting consumption from personal disposable income: it is not measured in its own right.

5. Which two statistics are needed in order to calculate velocity of circulation?

APPLYING ECONOMIC PRINCIPLES

1. With reference to Figure 30.1: (a) (i) Explain, with examples, the difference between 'liquid' and 'illiquid' assets. (ii) Explain the difference between 'narrow' measures of the money supply like M1, and 'broad' measures like M5. (b) M0 includes one of the items shown in the data, and one item not shown in the data. Identify each of these components. (c) Why does the government consider it necessary to have several different measures of the money supply? (d) Explain how a rise in bank lending can lead to an increase in M3.

2. With reference to Figure 30.3: (a) Describe the trends shown. (b) Explain the possible reasons for the trends shown.

3. (a) What is the 'quantity theory of money'? (b) With reference to Figures 30.1, 30.2 and 30.5, what does the data suggest about the validity of the assumptions and predictions of the quantity theory? Explain your answer.

4. (a) Define (i) exogenous money supply and (ii) endogenous money supply. (b) If the money supply is endogenous, does this imply that governments need not worry if expansionary policies increase the money supply? Explain your answer.

5. Refer to Figure 30.4. (a) What is meant by 'overfunding'? (b) (i) In what years was the PSBR overfunded? (ii) What was the value of net sterling lending by banks to the public sector in 1980? (c) Explain how overfunding can reduce the money supply. (d) What is the effect on the money supply of financing the PSBR by bank borrowing? Explain your answer. (e) What objections would monetarists have to an expansionary fiscal policy financed (i) by the sale of Treasury bills to banks, (ii) by gilt sales to the non bank public sector?

6. (a) Define 'supply-side economics' in relation to monetarist theory. (b) What is the relationship between the quantity theory and supply-side economics? (c) What alternative supply-side policies are there to monetarist policies? (d) Why is consideration of the 'supply side' important when attempting to devise non-inflationary expansionary policies?

FOR FURTHER INVESTIGATION
Figures on the money supply in the UK and the USA are published each month and widely reported in newspapers. The reasons for changes in the money supply are extensively analysed, and the changes themselves may have significant effects on other key economic variables. Keep a record of changes in the money supply over an extended period, and write a report which analyses the reasons for the changes and their effects on the rest of the economy.

ESSAYS
Refer to the data wherever possible, especially in the first essay.
1. To what extent can it be said that a contractionary monetary policy was the main reason for a reduction in inflation in the UK in the 1980s?
2. 'In order to reduce inflation further, the Government intends to continue reducing rates of monetary growth'. (*Financial Statement and Budget Report*, HMSO, March, 1984). Discuss the economic reasoning behind this statement. [Oxford 6/86]

The more the merrier

	No. of references	No. abandoned during investigation	Blocked	Cleared		
				Failed takeover	Successful takeover	
1980	5	1	1	0	3	1. Blue Circle Industries/ Armitage Shanks 2. S & W Berisford/ British Sugar Corporation 3. Compagnie Internationale Europcar/Godfrey Davis
1981	8	1	5	0	2	1. BTR/Serck 2. British Rail Hovercraft/ Hoverlloyd
1982	10	2	4	2	2	1. Nabisco Brands/ Huntley & Palmer Food 2. ICI/Arthur Holden
1983	9	2	4	3	0	
1984	4	1	0	2	1	1. British Electric Traction/ Initial

Source: *The Economist* 25 January 1986

Figure 31.2

What is meant by 'the public interest'?

84. (1) In determining for any purposes to which this section applies whether any particular matter operates, or may be expected to operate, against the public interest, the Commission shall take into account all matters which appear to them in the particular circumstances to be relevant and, among other things, shall have regard to the desirability—

(a) of maintaining and promoting effective competition between persons supplying goods and services in the United Kingdom;

(b) of promoting the interests of consumers, purchasers and other users of goods and services in the United Kingdom in respect of the prices charged for them and in respect of their quality and the variety of goods and services supplied;

(c) of promoting, through competition, the reduction of costs and the development and use of new techniques and new products, and of facilitating the entry of new competitors into existing markets;

(d) of maintaining and promoting the balanced distribution of industry and employment in the United Kingdom; and

(e) of maintaining and promoting activity in markets outside the United Kingdom on the part of producers of goods, and of suppliers of goods and services, in the United Kingdom.

Source: Fair Trading Act 1973

Figure 31.3

The BA/BCal merger: The Monopolies Commission goes on trial

FEW DECISIONS have damaged the reputation of the Monopolies and Mergers Commission as much as its approval of a merger between British Airways and British Caledonian, a deal finally accepted this week by the BCal board.

The British Airways/British Caledonian case has weakened the Commission's reputation for independence. It has also demonstrated some of the disadvantages of using a "public interest" criterion for such decisions, and of leaving the Commission to determine what constitutes the "public interest" in each case. It came close, in its decision on British Airways, to equating the "public interest" with BA's share of the world market. This naive mercantilist approach is traditional among airlines, but an investigating agency that is required to seek out the public interest might be expected to have adopted some more sophisticated concept.

The Commission is required to take account of all matters which appear relevant in the particular circumstances of a case when deciding whether a merger or monopoly may be contrary to the public interest. But it is also enjoined to consider the effect on competition and on consumers, on the regional distribution of industry and on exports; and Lord Young, the Secretary of State for Trade and Industry recently confirmed that he will follow the policy of his predecessor, Mr Norman Tebbit, by referring mergers to the Commission primarily because of their potential effect on competition.

The Commission has thus been told to consider the effect of mergers on competition, but it can consider any other factor it likes in judging the "public interest". It has been given this discretion because governments have not had enough faith in the benefits of competition to make its preservation the specific objective of competition policy.

If it is accepted that competition usually improves economic efficiency and that competition policy should therefore be dedicated to maintaining competition wherever it is appropriate, the criteria for judging the merits of mergers and monopolies would simply be whether a merger would reduce competition; and if it did, whether there were offsetting benefits which outweighed the potential losses.

Source: Adapted from *Financial Times* 23 December 1987

Figure 31.4

Bidders face takeover inquiry costs

THE Department of Trade & Industry is studying proposals that companies involved in takeovers and mergers should contribute some of the costs of Office of Fair Trading and Monopolies & Mergers Commission investigations.

This radical suggestion has been put forward as part of the wide-ranging review of the two DTI agencies by a committee headed by chief economist Hans Leisner.

The recent White Paper on the DTI covered legislative changes within the organisation, but an interim report on structural changes (not requiring changes in the law) is expected to be published shortly.

Exactly how companies would be charged for OFT and MMC investigations has not been decided, but the major cost burden would certainly fall on the bidder. Certainly a flexible scale of charges would be required, because different types of merger need different levels of investigation.

The DTI has been studying a report from management consultants Ernst & Whinney which examined the efficiency of the whole competition bureaucracy and has decreed, through last month's White Paper, that the process of examining mergers is to be speeded up.

Source: *Observer* 14 February 1988

Figure 31.1
Information may be missing from data, but no reference to this fact may be made in the data. Information may be included or excluded from data for a variety of reasons. For example, information on the composition of the Retail Prices Index may exclude certain items for the purpose of giving prominence to other items.

1. The data refers to only part of the work of the Monopolies and Mergers Commission (MMC). What type of references to the Commission have been omitted from the table?

Figure 31.2
It may be very difficult to put precise definitions on economic terms. Economists and politicians may wish to give precise definitions to terms, but this may prove very difficult in practice, e.g. in the case 'competition' or 'efficiency'. The inability to define terms precisely causes problems for the government when it is trying to frame legislation.

2. Which phrase suggests that the Fair Trading Act acknowledges the difficulty of setting out for the MMC all the circumstances under which a merger or takeover could be 'in the public interest'?

3. (a) Write down a phrase from either paragraph (a) or (d) of the Act which has not got a precise meaning. (b) Give two possible alternative meanings of the phrase.

Figure 31.3
Writers often express a point of view which should not be taken as objective fact. Some articles in newspapers attempt to present 'the facts' without expressing an opinion on them. Other articles analyse the facts, and attempt to form an opinion. It should not be assumed that the opinion presented will necessarily be 'balanced'. It should also not be assumed that there is anything wrong with a writer taking a clear position on a subject: often the most interesting and stimulating articles are those that take a clear position on an issue.

4. Write out a phrase or sentence that suggests that the writer was critical of the MMC decision.

Figure 31.4
An understanding of the role of economic institutions is necessary for the understanding of economic policy and processes. A very large number of organisations and institutions are involved in economic policy making and policy implementation. It is necessary to understand their role in order to understand the process of economic policy. For example, an understanding of control of the money supply requires an understanding of the role of commercial banks, the Bank of England and discount houses.

5. Describe the role in implementing competition policy of (a) the DTI, and (b) the OFT.

APPLYING ECONOMIC PRINCIPLES

1. Refer to Figure 31.1 (a) In 1984 there were about 500 acquisitions of UK public and private companies. Approximately what percentage came before the MMC? (b) How many references went to the MMC between 1980 and 1984? (c) What percentage were (i) abandoned during the investigation, (ii) blocked by the MMC? (d) What percentage of those that were cleared ended as successful takeovers? (e) For what reasons might the MMC deal with so few cases?

2. Using examples from Figure 31.1, explain how the following types of merger can lead to the growth of monopoly power in a market: (a) horizontal integration, (b) conglomerate integration.

3. With reference to Figures 31.2 and 31.3, what economic arguments might there be (a) for, (b) against equating 'the public interest' with BA's share of the world market?

4. (a) Figure 31.3 states that 'competition usually improves efficiency'. With reference to both technical and allocative efficiency, draw a diagram or diagrams to show the economic theory behind this statement. (b) Draw a diagram to show the circumstances under which less competition in a market can lead to greater economic efficiency.

5. Policies may be described as either discretionary or non-discretionary. Discretionary policies are adapted to changing circumstances whereas the aim of non-discretionary policies is to fix targets and direct policies to achieving those targets irrespective of short-term changes. (a) Why is present UK policy on mergers sometimes described as discretionary policy? (b) Using your knowledge of economic theory, and with reference to Figure 31.2 assess the costs and benefits of prohibiting all mergers which produce a market share of greater than 25 per cent. (c) If you were an economic adviser and were asked by the government to suggest revised criteria for competition policy, what would you suggest, and why?

6. With reference to Figure 31.4: (a) Explain the proposal for the changes in competition policy put forward by the committee headed by Hans Leisner. (b) (i) What is meant by 'external costs'? (ii) Explain how the proposals could be said to internalize external costs.

7. (a) As a result of restrictive practices in a market, the supply of a good is reduced. Draw a supply and demand diagram to show the effect on price and output of the formation of a cartel which restricts supply. (b) Explain why the elasticity of demand for a product is relevant to producers when deciding whether or not to restrict output.

FOR FURTHER INVESTIGATION
Reports of major takeover bids appear fairly frequently on the television and in the newspapers. Keep an account of those that refer to the government's policy on competition, monopoly and mergers. Write a report on one of the bids, bringing out the issues involved. Explain whether the bid was or was not referred to the MMC, and what factors lay behind the decision to make or not to make a reference.

ESSAYS
Refer to the data wherever possible, especially in the first essay.
1. 'The MMC has no useful role to play in competition policy because its terms of reference are so vague and it can deal with so few cases.' Discuss.
2. Discuss the problems involved in assessing the net benefit of a merger. [SUJB 6/85]

Selling the family silver

Figure 32.1
How privatized shares have performed

Company	Issue price	Price low	Price high	Current price	Issue yield	Current yield
Amersham International	142p (2/82)	142p (2/82)	645p (2/87)	538p	-3.5%	1.8%
Associated British Ports —first tranche	112p (2/83)	112p (2/83)	508p (3/87)	495p	8.9%	1.4%
—second tranche[1]	270p (4/84)	163p (12/84)	"	"	4.5%	
British Aerospace —first tranche	150p (2/81)	150p (2/81)	688p (3/87)	641p	7.4%	3.9%
—second tranche	375p (5/85)	295p (7/85)	"	"	5.2%	"
British Airways	65p (part-paid) (2/87)	65p (2/87)	131½p (4/87)	128p	6.8%	4.5%
British Gas	50p (part-paid) (11/86)	50p (11/86)	97½ (3/87)	90p	6.8%	5.3%
British Petroleum —first tranche	363p (10/79)	254p (9/81)	937p (3/87)	913p		5.4%
—second tranche	435p (9/83)	388p (12/83)	"	"		"
British Telecom	130p (11/84)	130p (11/84)	278p (4/86)	251p	9.3%	4.2%
Britoil —first tranche	215p (11/82)	101p (7/86)	275p (3/87)	246p	5.98%	4.6%
—second tranche	105p (8/85)	"	"	"	10%	"
Cable & Wireless —first tranche	168p (10/81)	168p (10/81)	388p (2/87)	376p	5.4%	1.8%
—second tranche	275p (12/83)	275p (12/83)	"	"	3.0%	"
—third tranche[2]	587p (12/85)	277p (9/86)	"	"	2.5%	"
Enterprise Oil	185p (6/84)	94p (7/86)	278p (3/87)	263p	5.4%	4.6%
Jaguar	165p (7/84)	165p (7/84)	628p (2/87)	578p	6.7%	2.3%

[1] 1986—One for one scrip issue. [2] 1986—One for one scrip issue.

Source: Datastream and *Observer* 5 April 1987

Figure 32.2

Comparing the efficiency of public and private enterprises

Comparisons are not straightforward.
(1) Few goods and services are provided by *both* the public and private sector (particularly in the UK).
(2) Many public corporations have some non-commercial objectives.

This means that profitability is not generally a good measure of performance. Comparisons therefore need to be made in terms of unit costs, productivity, efficiency in service to customers and similar measures. Even here there are difficulties: public corporations may face different input prices (for example, access to cheap finance) to those faced by private enterprises.

The most comprehensive comparison of public and private enterprises in the UK is that carried out by Pryke (1982). He was able to compare three activities where services were provided by both the public and private sector — airlines, ferries and hovercraft, and the sale of gas and electricity appliances. In each case Pryke's analysis showed a picture of a more profitable private enterprise increasing its market share at the expense of the public sector. Comparisons of costs and productivity show the private enterprises in a favourable light. Pryke concludes that the public enterprises he studied have been badly managed and that the main explanation for this poor performance is a weakening of incentives resulting from public ownership. That the performance of some parts of the public sector has been (to use Mr Moore's phrase) 'third-rate' appears indisputable. Some of the Commission's findings confirm this view (see, in particular, the reports on London Transport and on Postal Services).

However, when we look at the whole range of studies (including studies in other countries) which have compared efficiency of public and private provision, it is far from clear that private enterprise is always better than public enterprise. In many countries, and particularly the US, there is often a greater mix of public and private suppliers (for example, in electricity generating) than in the UK, and this makes comparisons easier. However, no clear conclusions emerge: in some cases private enterprises are found to be more efficient than their public counterparts (echoing Pryke's findings in the UK). But in other cases public enterprises are found to be more efficient.

Thus it does not seem that there is anything inherently superior about performance under private ownership. A recent study of the costs of refuse collection services in the UK emphasises the diversity of the efficiency of public suppliers in different locations (Audit Commission 1984). It is clear from that analysis that an efficient supplier (public or private) should be able to undercut substantially the costs incurred by the least efficient local authorities. But the Commission also concluded that the most effective local authorities (the top 25%) achieved cost levels as low as those of the private contractors they investigated.

Source: *The Economic Review* January, 1986

Figure 32.3

Does the private sector do better?

The whole policy of privatisation hinges on one big question: does being in the private sector inspire companies to do better?

Superficially, the signs are convincing. The National Freight Consortium, which was bought by its employees from the government in February 1982, has more than doubled its trading profits—and the value of its shares has increased 12-fold in three years. In preparing for privatisation, British Airways has converted its 1981–82 loss of £545m (inflated by redundancy provisions and increased depreciation in an effort to wipe clean its slate) into a string of profits.

However, the evidence is not overwhelming. Several companies (eg. Britoil, British Telecom, Cable and Wireless and Amersham) were making healthy profits under state ownership; and all have benefited from the 1980–81 growth in demand since the 1980–81 recession. Moreover, there have been failures: an employee buy-out of the Readhead's shipyard from British Shipbuilders in 1983 ended in liquidation earlier this year; and Associated British Ports, which almost trebled its profits in its first year in the private sector, lost £6.4m before tax in its latest financial year.

Source: *The Economist* 19 October 1985

Figure 32.1
Important statistics can often be calculated from other statistics. Figures presented in statistics can often be used to calculate other figures which are not shown. For example, newspapers frequently quote the figures for the balance of payments on current account, and the balance of trade: the invisible balance can be calculated from these statistics.

1. Calculate the last dividend paid before 5 April 1987 for British Telecom.

2. What percentage of all the issues shown might be under-subscribed ?

Figure 32.2
Academic studies may yield conflicting results. It may be tempting to accept the result of a study by an official institution or other respected institution as the 'truth'. There are many cases, however, where different studies produce different answers to the same question. The problem is especially acute in economics because data cannot usually be obtained experimentally. Disputes can arise not only in respect of the interpretation of evidence, but also as a result of the choice of data, and the method of collection employed.

3. What is Pryke's conclusion on the performance of the public enterprises that he studied?

4. Why does the writer of the article question Pryke's conclusion?

Figure 32.3
Figures considered in one context may give a different impression in another context. Politicians frequently quote figures to support particular policies, and often politicians of opposite persuasions will use the same figures to make different points. The impression given by a set of figures often depends upon the context in which they are used. For example, the fall in UK unemployment during 1987 and 1988 may look very impressive in isolation, but may look far less impressive when compared to the very sharp rise in unemployment in the early 1980s.

5. Name a context in which the doubling of trading profits of the National Freight Consortium would look less impressive than it appears in the article.

APPLYING ECONOMIC PRINCIPLES

1. Some economists have suggested that the term 'privatization' can cover a range of different policies such as (a) denationalization, (b) liberalization or deregulation, (c) encouraging private provision. Explain the meaning of each of these terms.

2. With reference to Figure 32.1: (a) Do the data suggest that privatization issues were generally underpriced? Explain your answer. (b) For what (i) economic reasons, and (ii) political reasons might a privatization share issue be underpriced?

3. Critics of privatization say that the policy often creates private monopolies out of public monopolies. (a) What is meant by a 'monopoly'? (b) What is a 'natural monopoly'? (c) List two industries in Figure 32.1 in which there are natural monopolies. (d) Will a privatized monopoly necessarily be more efficient than a publicly owned monopoly? Explain your answer.

4. The UK Government in the 1980s has claimed that privately owned industries are usually more efficient. Refer to Figures 32.2 and 32.3. (a) What is meant by 'efficiency'? (b) List three ways suggested by the articles in which efficiency can be measured. (c) What problems are involved in comparing the efficiency of public and private enterprises?

5. (a) What is an 'employee buy-out'? (b) What evidence does Figure 32.3 provide on the effectiveness of employee buy-outs of public enterprises? (c) For what reasons might employee buy-outs be (i) more successful, and (ii) less successful than stock market issues as forms of privatization?

6. A major reason for the privatization programme has been to reduce the size of the PSBR. (a) What is the PSBR? (b) Why might a government want to reduce the PSBR? (c) The government has sold off some profit-making public sector businesses. Will privatization reduce the PSBR in the long-term? Explain your answer.

7. Supporters of nationalized industries in areas such as the supply of gas and water argue that the state will be more concerned than private industry about external costs. (a) What is meant by 'external costs'? (b) Why might private firms ignore the external costs of their activities? (c) What could be the external costs of a privatized water industry failing to spend sufficient on providing clean water? (d) (i) Under what circumstances might public sector enterprises fail to take external costs into account? (ii) Under what circumstances might private sector enterprises take action to reduce the external costs of their activities?

8. What information would help economists to assess the costs and benefits of privatization?

FOR FURTHER INVESTIGATION
Over the next few months follow the share prices of three of the industries in Figure 32.1. Plot the prices on graph paper. Also plot the figures for the FT 100 Index on the same graph paper. Write a summary of your findings, including the answer to the following questions. Is there any relationship between the performance of shares in denationalized industries? Do your findings suggest that the gains in the value of shares in denationalized industries were a once-and-for-all gain accruing to the original purchasers, or are they still outperforming other shares?

ESSAYS
Refer to the data wherever possible, especially in the first essay.

1. A former Prime Minister, Harold Macmillan, compared the sale of state assets to 'selling the family silver' (a) What is meant by the phrase 'selling the family silver'? (b) To what extent is it a fair criticism of the government's privatization programme in the 1980s?

2. (a) Explain the meaning of the term 'privatization'. (b) What have been the objectives of the Government's privatization policy? (c) Discuss the likelihood of achieving these objectives, and the extent to which the privatization policy may have adverse consequences. [SUJB 6/86]

Taking work to the workers

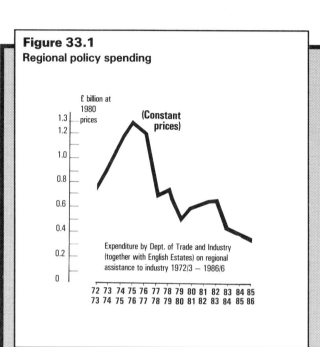

Figure 33.1
Regional policy spending

£ billion at 1980 prices

(Constant prices)

Expenditure by Dept. of Trade and Industry (together with English Estates) on regional assistance to industry 1972/3 — 1986/6

72/73 73/74 74/75 75/76 76/77 77/78 78/79 79/80 80/81 81/82 82/83 83/84 84/85 85/86

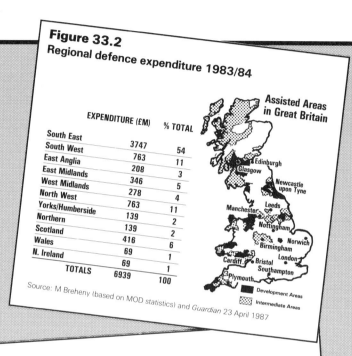

Figure 33.2
Regional defence expenditure 1983/84

	EXPENDITURE (£M)	% TOTAL
South East	3747	54
South West	763	11
East Anglia	208	3
East Midlands	346	5
West Midlands	278	4
North West	763	11
Yorks/Humberside	139	2
Northern	139	2
Scotland	416	6
Wales	69	1
N. Ireland	69	1
TOTALS	**6939**	**100**

Assisted Areas in Great Britain

Edinburgh
Glasgow
Newcastle upon Tyne
Manchester
Leeds
Nottingham
Birmingham
Norwich
Cardiff
Bristol
London
Southampton
Plymouth

■ Development Areas
▨ Intermediate Areas

Source: M Breheny (based on MOD statistics) and *Guardian* 23 April 1987

Figure 33.3

Automatic development grants go

"YOU SHOULD be in no doubt about our concern to encourage competitive companies in manufacturing and service industries throughout Britain, and I stress, throughout Britain. That is best achieved not by a sectoral approach to industry and not by automatic grants but by working with private enterprise in encouraging management to develop their skills".

Thus Lord Young, in a speech delivered in Manchester shortly after he launched the Department of Trade and Industry as the department for Enterprise, explained the reasons for the new emphasis in regional policy.

The main features of the new policy are:-

■ Companies in the assisted areas will not be able to apply for the virtually automatic regional development grant after March 31 1988.

■ Regional selective assistance, whereby companies have to demonstrate that their planned investment would not go ahead without Government money will continue to be available.

■ Companies in the assisted areas employing fewer than 25 people will be able to apply for two new grants from April 1. One is an investment grant of 15 per cent towards the cost of fixed assets subject to a maximum grant of £15,000. The other is an innovation grant of 50 per cent to support product and process development subject ot a maximum grant of £25,000.

■ Two thirds of the cost of consultancy services available to companies employing fewer than 500 people will be met by the DTI. Services will be available covering design, marketing, quality management, manufacturing systems, and from April, business planning, and financial and information systems.

■ The assisted areas map, covering development and intermediate areas, will be unchanged for the lifetime of this Parliament.

■ The new grants, and help towards the costs of consultancy services, will also be available in the Urban Programme areas. (In other parts of the country, the Government will meet one half of the cost).

The Government's objective for the regions is unchanged from the December 1983 statement, namely "to encourage the development of indigenous potential within the assisted areas with the long-term objective of self-generating growth in these areas."

The January White Paper, however, says that the Government believes this objective will be achieved more effectively by ensuring that the main aims of its enterprise policies "are properly reflected in the regions".

The new thrust of regional policy, therefore, is to encourage the expansion of small and medium-sized companies, while maintaining the means to attract larger-scale investment.

Source: *Financial Times* 28 January 1988

Figure 33.1
Values may be expressed in real or money terms. A rise in the value of a variable does not necessarily represent a rise in its real value unless allowance is made for inflation. Figures are therefore often adjusted to remove purely inflationary rises in value. For example, the national income is often expressed at constant prices in order to remove increases caused merely by price movements, so that increases in its real value can be identified.
1. Explain the method of adjusting for inflation used here.
2. If the figures had been expressed in current prices, how would the shape of the curve be affected? Explain your answer.

Figure 33.2
Population is not distributed equally throughout the UK, and this will affect the interpretation of certain data. The country is divided into standard regions for the purpose of producing economic data. There are significant differences in the population of the regions, however, and therefore care must be taken when studying statistics based on them. For example, if unemployment figures (in thousands) were produced for different regions, the South East would appear high on the list: the unemployment rate, which measures unemployment as a percentage of the working population in different regions, would provide a much more meaningful figure.
3. In 1984 the population of the South East was 17 112 000 and the population of the North West was 6 396 000. Calculate the regional defence spending per head for (a) the South East, and (b) the North West.
4. Would it have been preferable for the regional defence expenditure figures to have been presented on a per capita basis? Explain your answer.

Figure 33.3
Newspaper and magazine articles may attempt to report 'the facts', or they may attempt to analyse information and express opinions. Newspaper articles on economic issues can often be categorized as one of two types: the first type tries to report the facts (although what facts newspapers choose to report may reflect an opinion); the second type may try to analyse and evaluate the facts, often taking a particular point of view. For example, one newspaper article could reproduce official figures on unemployment whereas another article may attempt to explain the figures, analyse their economic effects, and comment on whether they are 'good' or 'bad'.
5. Does this article generally attempt to report facts, or to analyse and evaluate them? Explain your answer.

APPLYING ECONOMIC PRINCIPLES

1. With reference to Figure 33.1: (a) Describe the trends shown in the data. (b) Explain the possible reasons for these trends. (c) What are the possible economic consequences of a real decline in regional policy spending?

2. Refer to Figure 33.2. (a) What do the data suggest about the allocation of government contracts on defence between the assisted and non-assisted areas? (Use the map to help you identify assisted and non-assisted areas.) (b) Should the government change its defence procurement as a regional policy measure to assist regions in industrial decline? Explain your answer.

3. With reference to Figure 33.3: (a) Describe the main changes in regional policy announced in January 1988. (b) For what reasons were these changes introduced? (c) Why do some economists consider that regional policy is limited in effect unless it is also tied to improvements in infrastructure in depressed regions?

4. Firms are often reluctant to move to depressed areas of the country because costs of production are higher than in other regions. (a) What is meant by 'external economies of scale', sometimes called 'economies of concentration'? (b) What external economies of scale could be forgone by a car firm setting up in an assisted area in which there had been no car industry previously, as opposed to setting up in a traditional car manufacturing area?. (c) Explain why a firm with high capital costs in a depressed region might experience a sharp rise in average fixed costs as a result of a drop in the demand for its products. (d) (i) Do regional development grants for buildings reduce fixed or variable costs? Explain your answer. (ii) What difficulties might a firm experience when a regional development grant has been used up?

5. (a) What is the 'principle of comparative advantage'? (b) Explain how regional policy may cause a distribution of industry in the UK which is contrary to this principle. (c) How could massive regional expenditure help to cancel out the cost disadvantages of a region over a long period of time? (d) What external benefits could arise following a sharp increase in regional policy spending in areas with very high unemployment: (i) in assisted areas; (ii) in non-assisted areas?

FOR FURTHER INVESTIGATION
Newspapers frequently carry advertisements for different areas and regions of the country. Peterborough and Corby, for example, have advertised extensively in recent years. Collect some samples of such advertisements and obtain copies of any information that they offer. List the incentives that the different places offer, and mark clearly which are offered as part of regional policy. Try also to identify incentives that arise as a result of other initiatives, e.g. enterprise zones and local enterprise boards.

ESSAYS
Refer to the data wherever possible, especially in the first answer.
1. Describe and evaluate the approach of the Conservative Government to regional policy in the 1980s.
2. 'Regional policy is necessary because the free market is not the appropriate method of distributing industry throughout the country.' Discuss.

Delivering the goods

Figure 34.1
Some indicators of economic growth

| | UK ECONOMY | | | | | | WORLD ECONOMY | | |
	Real GDP % change		Manufacturing output (% change)	Unemployment 4th qtr millions	Retail price index 4th qtr % change	Current balance £bn	PSBR £bn	Real GNP	Consumer prices (% change)	World trade
	Total	Non-oil								
1986	2.0	2.9	0.8	3.1	3.4	-0.1	3.3	2.5	2.1	4.7
1987	3.3	3.6	4.0	2.8	3.8	-1.1	3.7	2.3	3.2	3.3
1988	2.2	2.7	1.5	2.7	4.9	-3.4	1.3	2.5	3.4	3.3

Source: *Financial Times* 20 August 1987

Figure 34.2
Output per head in the major 7 industrialized countries

(Average annual % change)

	Manufacturing			Whole economy		
	1964–73	1973–79	1979–86H1	1964–73	1973–79	1979–86H1
United States	3.4	3.5	2.3	1.6	0.2	0.7
Japan	9.8	4.0	2.7	7.4	2.9	2.8
West Germany	3.9	3.3	2.3	4.2	2.9	1.4
France*	5.4	3.0	2.5	4.5	2.8	1.5
UK	3.8	0.7	3.5	2.7	1.1	1.9
Italy*	5.5	2.5	2.4	5.6	1.7	1.0
Canada	4.3	2.5	3.0	2.5	0.5	0.6
Average of major 7†	5.0	3.2	2.5	3.6	1.5	1.3

*For whole of industry, not just manufacturing.
†Weighted on basis of 1980 manufacturing output, at 1980 exchange rates.
(**H1** = First Half)

Source: OECD and *Economic Progress Report* (Treasury)

Figure 34.3
Falling short

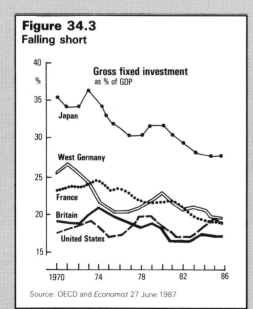

Gross fixed investment as % of GDP

Japan — West Germany — France — Britain — United States

Source: OECD and *Economist* 27 June 1987

Figure 34.4

Risk of overheating 'exaggerated'

RECENT FEARS that the British economy might be in danger of overheating are exaggerated and the parallels drawn with the boom of the early 1970s misleading, according to the National Institute of Economic and Social Research.

In its latest economic review, the institute said it would not characterise the present period of relatively fast economic growth as a boom since, although demand is strong, that buoyancy rests mainly on sharp growth in real earnings rather than the expansion of credit.

The growth of earnings, in turn, owes much to a sustained improvement in productivity growth and better terms of trade rather than to an excess demand for labour forcing companies to concede large pay increases.

The institute said the surprising feature of the present upturn was the weakness of both fixed investment demand and stock building, although it expected a modest recovery in investment this year or next. That should help to sustain a growth rate that would otherwise be quite sharply cut back.

The institute forecasts output growth this year of 3 per cent to 3½ per cent, slowing to 2 per cent to 2½ per cent in 1988. The forecasts are slightly above those in the institute's economic review in May.

Source: *Financial Times* 20 August 1987

Figure 34.1
Some economic variables are not measurable in themselves. The government has fairly precise ways of measuring some key economic variables. The Retail Prices Index, for example, is widely regarded as a good measure of consumer price inflation. Other variables, such as economic growth, are not directly measurable, and a variety of other variables may be used to try and measure them.

1. (a) Describe what happened between 1986 and 1988 to UK (i) real GDP, (ii) Retail Prices Index, and (iii) PSBR. (b) Explain how each of the variables in (a) may be related to the level of economic growth.

2. Explain how the current account of the balance of payments might be a good indicator of economic growth if one country is growing faster than its main trading partners, but a poor indicator of economic growth if all the countries are tending to grow at the same rate.

Figure 34.2
Years may be divided into time periods for the purpose of analysing trends. When comparisons need to be made over a large number of years, years may be divided into time periods to make it easier to identify trends. These periods may not necessarily be of equal length, but they may exhibit common features. For example, population growth may be looked at by comparing the almost 700-year period between 1066 and 1750 with the 50 years that followed. The first period would approximately represent the years between the Domesday Book and the Industrial Revolution, when population change was very slow.

3. What significant world economic event occurred in 1973 and again in 1979, which would account for the choice of periods shown?

4. In terms of economic growth, describe the differences between the three periods shown.

Figure 34.3
Figures may be presented in a 'gross' or 'net' form. A net figure suggests that something has been deducted from a gross, or unmodified, figure. For example, gross income refers to income before deductions like income tax have been made, whereas net income refers to income after deductions.

5. What is deducted from gross fixed investment to give net fixed investment?

6. Can it be inferred from the figures that over 25 per cent of Japanese GDP was devoted to increasing its capital stock in 1986? Explain your answer.

Figure 34.4
Economic analysts will differ in their opinions according to the economic indicators selected for analysis. People sometimes criticize economists because they come to different conclusions on the same subject. Such criticisms are often ill-informed because economists have to reach their conclusions using a wide variety of data which may be capable of different, often contradictory interpretations.

7. What evidence is there in the passage to suggest that the National Institute of Economic and Social Research is interpreting indicators about the position of the economy differently from some other forecasters?

APPLYING ECONOMIC PRINCIPLES

1. (a) Economic growth can refer to a growth in productive potential. Illustrate this interpretation of economic growth on a production possibility frontier diagram. (b) What alternative interpretation of economic growth is suggested by the data in this unit?

2. (a) (i) What is meant by the 'trade cycle'? (ii) Describe the conditions that would characterise the top (or 'boom' period) of the trade cycle. Refer to Figure 34.1. (b) What evidence is shown to suggest that the UK was experiencing an economic boom in 1987? (c) Assess the contribution of (i) North Sea oil, and (ii) manufacturing output to economic growth in the three years shown. (d) What evidence suggests that the economic condition in 1987 might have been leading to problems in 1988?

3. Refer to Figures 34.2 and 34.3. (a) Which economy had the fastest rate of productivity growth in the three time periods shown in Figure 34.2? (b) What appears to be the major reason for that economy's economic success?

4. (a) Refer to Figure 34.4. Why did the National Institute of Economic and Social Research doubt that the UK was in an economic boom in 1988? (b) Explain how a growth in productivity could cause economic growth without increasing inflation. Use a diagram to illustrate your answer. (c) (i) With reference to Figure 34.3, can it be inferred that the growth in productivity was caused mainly by a growth in investment? (ii) What other factors could cause a growth in productivity?

5. (a) What policies to promote economic growth might be favoured by an economist who holds neo-classical views about the operation of the economy? (b) What policies to promote economic growth might be favoured by an economist who holds Keynesian views about the operation of the economy? (c) Use a diagram or diagrams to show the circumstances under which the Keynesian policy might lead to (i) more economic growth, and (ii) stagflation.

6. What is meant by the 'external costs' of economic growth? (b) Explain some of the ways in which economic growth might lead to (i) more pollution, and (ii) less pollution. (c) Describe three policies that the government could use to reduce the costs of pollution.

FOR FURTHER ANALYSIS
Quality newspapers give a variety of statistics which can be used to assess the position of an economy on the trade cycle. Some of these are suggested in the data in this unit. Collect information on the economy over several months which may indicate the country's position on the trade cycle. Present the information in appropriate forms, e.g. tables, line graphs, etc. Write an analysis of the information, using the data to determine the position of the economy in relation to the trade cycle.

ESSAYS
Refer to the data wherever possible, especially in the first essay.

1. The economic growth rate of the UK has not improved over the last 25 years or so, the performance of other industrial nations has simply deteriorated relatively more rapidly.' Discuss.

2. Do the costs of economic growth outweigh the benefits? [London 6/85]

The most vicious circle

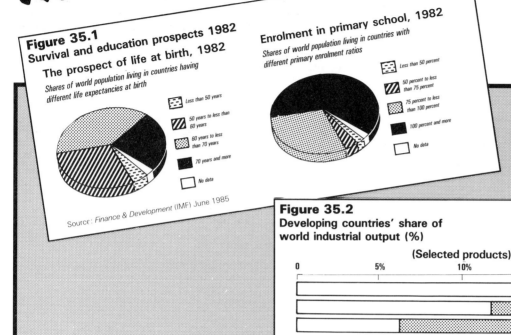

Figure 35.1
Survival and education prospects 1982
The prospect of life at birth, 1982

Shares of world population living in countries having different life expectancies at birth

- Less than 50 years
- 50 years to less than 60 years
- 60 years to less than 70 years
- 70 years and more
- No data

Enrolment in primary school, 1982

Shares of world population living in countries with different primary enrolment ratios

- Less than 50 percent
- 50 percent to less than 75 percent
- 75 percent to less than 100 percent
- 100 percent and more
- No data

Source: *Finance & Development* (IMF) June 1985

Figure 35.2
Developing countries' share of world industrial output (%)

(Selected products)

	0	5%	10%	15%	20%

- Textiles
- Footwear
- Iron & steel
- Paper & paper products
- Electrical & electronic products
- Professional & scientific equipment

☐ 1970   ▦ 1987

Source: *UNIDO and Economist* 6 December 1986

Figure 35.3

Worlds apart — and the gap continues to widen

There is to be a UN International Conference on Population in Mexico City next month. It is to mark 10 years since the first World Conference on Population in Bucharest in 1974. In those years those living on the planet have increased by 777 million, nine out of 10 of them in the developing countries of the world. In the rich developed countries population growth has almost halted.

The haves and the have-nots live in different worlds. The gap widens; in numbers of people, and in wealth. The millions are hard to comprehend. The additional 770 millions of the past decade are three times as many as the total population of the European Community.

As for the money, the average incomes of the high-income haves are 30 to 40 times as much as the low-income have-nots. A 1 per cent growth rate in GNP improves the lot of the Chinese, on average, by $3 and of Americans by $130 per head per year.

Source: *Guardian* 3 July 1984

Figure 35.4

Economic problems in Africa

In 1985 the problems of Africa have forced the developed world to recognize that a disaster of global dimensions has occurred. The World Bank estimates that 200 million people—60 per cent of Africa's total population—eat fewer calories than is necessary for a survival diet. In particular there are 30 million people seriously affected by food shortages and in urgent need of food aid.

Famine can be defined as existing when a group's access to food so completely collapses that mass starvation occurs. It is not merely a case of malnutrition, which has been an endemic problem for years. It is characterized by a radical change in behaviour in order to search for food. The present famine has created 10 million migrants. Famine is linked to long-term poverty, with a lack of purchasing power amongst the poor. Crop failure is a probable, but not inevitable, reason for this. Indeed there have been instances where

famine has persisted despite an increase in food production. However, in the African countries where food shortages are worst, food production per capita has been falling over the past fourteen years.

The latest drought in Africa was undoubtedly severe, but there is also an underlying problem. The Sahara desert has been encroaching southwards at the rate of 100 km a year as a result of deforestation and soil erosion. In the potentially fertile Sahel area on the southern fringe of the desert, food production has been declining for years. The problem has been compounded by governments tailoring their agricultural development programmes in favour of cash crops for export. In countries such as Mali, Burkina and Chad, cotton production has increased markedly—a tribute to its resistance to drought but also to the increase in its world price. This has had the effect of enticing farmers away from the staple

food crops of sorghum and millet.

The immediate response to the famine by the West was to step up donations of food aid. By March 1985 the UN estimates of emergency food requirements had reached 7 million tonnes. With commercial imports and non-emergency food aid of considerable proportions, as many as 40 per cent of Africans in countries south of the Sahara were living on foreign food in 1985. The logistics of imports on this scale are complex. Distribution requires mastery of Africa's inadequate infrastructure. Ethiopia required 1.5 million tonnes of food aid as a result of the famine, but her three ports can only handle 3500 tonnes a day. Even if the transportation problems are overcome, longer-term difficulties remain. The danger with food aid is that it creates a dependence on outside sources of food. By undermining the price of local food it can discourage production and prolong dependence.

Source: *British Economy Survey* Autumn 85

Figure 35.1
Economic data may require careful interpretation to avoid misunderstanding. Some data may not mean what they appear to mean at first glance. For example, if the number of people in a particular age group falls as a percentage of total population it does not necessarily mean that the absolute number of people in the age group has fallen.

1. Can it be inferred from the left-hand pie chart that in less than a quarter of countries in the world the life expectancy rate is 70 years or more? Explain your answer.

2. Can it be inferred from the right-hand pie chart that more than half the countries in the world have all their children at primary school? Explain your answer.

Figure 35.2
An increasing share of world output does not necessarily imply an increasing share of world exports. The developing world is increasing its production of many of the manufactured goods traditionally produced in the industrialized nations of the world. This does not automatically mean that the production of these goods in industrialized countries is falling or that their exports are declining.

3. Explain why the increase in the share of world output of textiles accounted for by developing countries does not *necessarily* mean that the UK share of the world textile exports has to fall.

4. Name one product group increasingly manufactured in the developed world which will not at present have a large domestic market and therefore will almost certainly threaten UK exports. Give reasons for your answer.

Figure 35.3
A high standard of living does not necessarily imply a high standard of general welfare. It is easy to fall into the trap of assuming that people who enjoy a high level of material wealth are much happier and have a much higher standard of general wellbeing than people with lower living standards. This may be the unintentional result of the type of language used in newspaper articles.

5. Which words used in the passage may seem to imply that higher material living standards necessarily mean increased general welfare?

Figure 35.4
The word 'distribution' has different meanings in economics in different contexts. Distribution can refer to the way in which income and wealth are distributed between economies or between people within an economy. It can also refer to the problems of actually getting goods and services from producers to consumers.

6. How is it suggested that the problems of Africa are partly problems of distribution in both senses of the word as defined above?

APPLYING ECONOMIC PRINCIPLES

1. With reference to Figure 35.1: (a) (i) Calculate approximately what percentage of the world's population in 1982 lived in countries with a life expectancy of less than 60 years. (ii) Calculate approximately what percentage of the world's population in 1982 lived in countries with a primary school enrolment rate of less than 75 per cent. (b) What other measures can be used to assess degrees of economic development?

2. (a) Developing countries traditionally have produced and exported primary products, and imported manufactured goods. Explain why this pattern occurred. With reference to Figure 35.2: (b) Describe how this traditional pattern is changing. (c) Explain, referring to the theory of comparative advantage, why these changes are occurring (i) very rapidly in the case of footwear, and (ii) more slowly in the case of professional and scientific equipment.

3. With reference to Figure 35.3: (a) Explain why the world can be said to be getting poorer. (b) Describe the effect that a 5 per cent economic growth rate would have on the incomes of the Chinese, and of the Americans. (c) Why is it highly unlikely that the Chinese will ever enjoy the same living standards as the Americans?

4. The creation of wealth requires the production of a surplus which can be channelled into the production and acquisition of capital. (a) With reference to Figure 35.4, explain how a switch from consumer goods to capital goods could involve a high opportunity cost for a developing country. (b) Explain how the provision of extra capital equipment in agriculture could increase (i) productivity, and (ii) wages in the agricultural sector. (c) Explain how higher wages in the agricultural sector will, via the multiplier, lead to an increase in incomes throughout an economy.

FOR FURTHER INVESTIGATION
In the early 1980s two important reports were published by the Brandt Commission on the relationship between the 'North', the world's wealthier nations, and the 'South', the world's poorer nations. The first Brandt Report was called *North-South: A Programme for Survival.* The second was called *Common Crisis: North-South: Co-operation for World Recovery.* The reports are fairly short, easy to understand, and widely available in libraries. Try to obtain copies of the reports, and write a brief summary of their main findings and recommendations. Make sure you try to find out why, according to the reports, the North cannot cut itself off from the problems of the South, and why the two parts of the world are interdependent.

ESSAYS
Refer to the data wherever possible, especially in the first essay.

1. (a) What are the main characteristics of the world's poorest nations? (b) Why do very poor countries, such as those in sub-Saharan Africa, find it so difficult to achieve economic growth? (c) How are some developing countries increasing their rates of economic growth?

2. How would you distinguish between the terms 'economic growth' and 'economic development'? Compare the possible effects of a policy of population control with either investment in manufacturing, or improvements in agriculture, on the standard of living in a less developed economy. [JMB 6/87]

A bad debt

Figure 36.1
Latin America's foreign debt

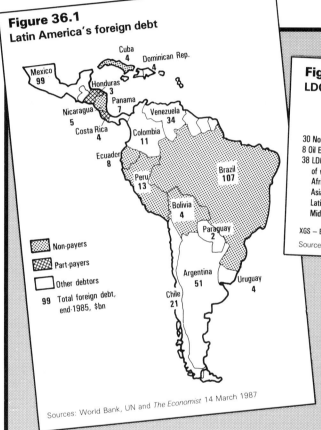

Non-payers

Part-payers

Other debtors

99 Total foreign debt, end-1985, $bn

Sources: World Bank, UN and *The Economist* 14 March 1987

Figure 36.2
LDCs — External Indicators

	Current Account ($bn)				Debt/XGS (%)			
	1984	1985	1986 (e)	1987 (f)	1984	1985	1986 (e)	1987 (f)
30 Non-oil LDCs	-19	-26	-13	-20	214	227	245	256
8 Oil Exporters	-1	0	-27	-22	153	169	255	247
38 LDCs	-20	-26	-40	-42	196	210	248	254
of which:								
Africa	-2	0	-6	-6	164	170	260	271
Asia	-4	-12	-1	-7	117	131	149	154
Latin America	3	-1	-11	-10	346	367	430	437
Middle East	-17	-13	-22	-21	69	74	91	97

XGS — Exports of goods and services; (e) — estimate; (f) — forecast

Source: Barclays Economics Department database *Barclays Bank Review* May 1987

Figure 36.3

Why do debt problems arise?

From this discussion it is possible to identify a number of broad reasons why debt problems emerge. First there may be factors that are exogenous to the debtor, such as falling export demand resulting from a world economic recession, or rising real world interest rates, or unfavourable changes in exchange rates between third countries. Second, debt may have been poorly managed with the borrower borrowing too much given the capacity of the economy to repay, failing to choose the most appropriate sources of finance (possibly borrowing over a shorter term and at a higher cost than necessary), and failing to collect adequate information about the debt position. Third, and in addition to poor debt management, the economy itself may have been poorly managed. Failure by governments to undertake measures to increase domestic savings, by, for example, repressing financial markets and preventing domestic real interest rates from rising above very low or even negative levels, or by resisting the opportunity of raising saving compulsorily through the fiscal system, is likely to mean that the savings gap will not be closed.

Furthermore reluctance to reduce exchange rates that are greatly overvalued or to encourage export promotion in other ways will mean that the foreign exchange gap will not be closed.

Source: *Economics* Summer 1985
(G. Bird: "Understanding International Debt")

Figure 36.4

LDC debt crisis: A new phase?

BRAZIL'S decision unilaterally to suspend interest payments on debt owed to commercial banks represents a major challenge to the framework so far used in handling the LDC debt crisis. The approach has consisted of three main components: first, a rescheduling of principal payments; second, the provision of new money to assist countries in meeting their interest payment; and lastly, the overseeing of economic adjustment programmes by the IMF. The Brazilian action challenges this approach in a number of respects. In the first place, it questions the ability of the existing arrangements to provide external finance in the amounts needed by debtor countries to support medium-term economic recovery. Secondly, it questions the basis on which new funds are to be provided if, as in the current case of Brazil, debtor countries refuse to submit to renewed IMF conditionality. More fundamentally, however, it once more brings into the centre of debate the issue of how the burden of adjustment is to be shared between, on the one hand, the debtor countries and, on the other, external creditors—in particular, developed country governments and the commercial banks.

Source: *Barclays Bank Review* May 1987

Figure 36.1
In order to assess the significance of an economic problem to a nation, additional information about the nation may be required. Countries may suffer 'problems' such as a balance of payments crisis, unemployment, or a high public sector borrowing requirement. The full significance of the problems can only be meaningfully assessed in relation to the size of, for example, the country's GDP, in order to put the problems in perspective.

1. Which country had the largest debt problem in 1987?

2. What additional information might help in the assessment of the significance of this country's debt problem?

Figure 36.2
The significance of an economic variable may be easier to assess if one variable is expressed as a percentage or ratio of another variable. Sometimes one piece of data is expressed as a ratio of another piece of data. For example, imports might be expressed as a percentage of home demand for a product to give a figure for import penetration.

3. What figure has debt been expressed as a percentage of, and why?

4. Name one other variable which debt could have been expressed as a percentage of in order to give more significance to the debt figure.

Figure 36.3
It is important to distinguish between fact and opinion in data. Economists frequently mix the reporting of facts with their own informed opinions about why problems have arisen and how they can be resolved. It is important to be able to distinguish fact from opinion.

5. Give one statement of fact from the passage, and one statement which represents the writer's opinion.

Figure 36.4
Initials are used increasingly in economic data. It is important to try and learn initials which occur frequently in data and which may rarely be written in full. Some can mean different things in different contexts; for example, NICs can stand for both National Insurance contributions or newly industrialized countries.

6. What do the initials LDC and IMF stand for?

APPLYING ECONOMIC PRINCIPLES

1. With reference to Figures 36.1 and 36.2: (a) Estimate (i) the total outstanding debt of Latin America at the end of 1985; (ii) the value of exports of goods and services of Latin America in 1985. (b) Do the current account figures for Latin America suggest that the debt to export ratio was likely to improve after 1987? Explain your answer.

2. (a) What is the difference between 'exogenous' factors and 'endogenous' factors? (b) With reference to Figure 36.3: Name one exogenous factor and one endogenous factor that have turned Third World debt into a major problem. (c) (i) What policy have debtor nations been pursuing in relation to their exchange rates? (ii) Why might they have chosen this policy? (iii) How might a different exchange rate policy have helped to ease the debt problem? (d) In addition to exchange rate policy, describe and explain the other policies that a debtor nation may employ to try and reduce its debt, according to the article.

3. With reference to Figure 36.4: (a) Explain the meaning of (i) 'rescheduling', (ii) 'adjustment programme', and (iii) 'medium term recovery'. (b) What factors could have influenced Brazil's decision to suspend interest payments? (c) What problems could arise for (i) debtors, and (ii) creditors following a default by a major debtor nation?

4. Explain whether the following are likely to improve or worsen the debt crisis, giving reasons for your answers: (a) a sharp increase in the price of primary products other than oil; (b) an economic slump in the developed world; (c) a sharp improvement in the terms of trade of debtor nations; (d) a large fall in world interest rates.

5. Debtor nations can use their loans in a number of ways. How would the following methods of using the loans affect the ability of debtor nations to repay in the longer-term. (a) an increase in spending on the military; (b) an increase in the import of investment goods; (c) an increase in spending on investment in agriculture; (d) a decrease in public borrowing and a fall in interest rates?

FOR FURTHER INVESTIGATION
Look for articles on the debt crisis in newspapers and magazines. Such articles may deal with the crisis in a number of different ways. For example, they may focus on individual countries or areas; they may look at the effect of the crisis on the banking system; or they may try to explain in general terms how the crisis has arisen and offer some possible solutions. Use the information to write a report indicating how the crisis is progressing, and how the debtor nations and lenders are dealing with the problem.

ESSAYS
Refer to the data wherever possible, especially in the first essay.

1. (a) How serious is the current international debt problem? (b) Why did international debt become a 'problem'? (c) What methods have been employed to deal with the debt problem?

2. 'The debt crisis has resulted from irresponsible lending by creditors and irresponsible use of loans by the debtor nations.' Discuss.

A helping hand?

Figure 37.1
Composition of net aid flows (US $ billions) 1983

	UK	USA	All OECD
TOTAL AID A + B	2.19	5.78	25.64
A Bilateral aid 1 + 2	1.33	4.32	18.28
1 Grants	1.33	3.16	13.18
Technical assistance	0.43	0.95	5.25
Food aid	0.03	0.43	0.85
2 Loans	–	1.15	5.10
Development loans	–	0.36	3.68
Food aid loans	–	0.69	1.00
B Multilateral aid	0.87	1.47	7.35
Food aid	0.15	0.14	1.09

Source: OECD Development Co-operation 1982 Review and *The Economic Review* January 1984.

Figure 37.2
OECD countries: Official Development Assistance (ODA) as a percentage of donor GNP

	1970	1975	1980	1985[a]
Italy	0.16	0.11	0.17	0.31
New Zealand	0.23	0.52	0.33	0.25
United Kingdom	0.41	0.39	0.35	0.33
Belgium	0.46	0.59	0.50	0.53
Austria	0.07	0.21	0.23	0.38
Netherlands	0.61	0.75	1.03	0.90
France	0.66	0.62	0.64	0.79
Japan	0.23	0.23	0.32	0.29
Finland	0.06	0.18	0.22	0.39
W. Germany	0.32	0.40	0.44	0.48
Denmark	0.38	0.58	0.74	0.80
Australia	0.59	0.65	0.48	0.49
Sweden	0.38	0.82	0.79	0.86
Canada	0.41	0.54	0.43	0.49
Norway	0.32	0.66	0.85	1.00
United States	0.32	0.27	0.27	0.24
Switzerland	0.15	0.19	0.24	0.31
All OECD countries	0.34	0.35	0.37	0.36

Note: (a) Preliminary estimates
Source: World Development Report 1986 and *The Economic Review* March 1987.

Figure 37.3

What do we mean by 'foreign aid'?

Foreign aid has acquired a somewhat dubious reputation because of the strictures of commentators who believe that capital transfers from developed to developing countries could better be managed by private direct investment or lending via international capital markets. Some of their criticisms are accurate but misrepresent the potential for alternative methods of capital transfer, while other criticisms are based on the fact that the 'aid' budgets of many countries include allocations of money for purposes quite unrelated to development assistance. The latter point may be illustrated by two examples.

(a) Appropriations for foreign aid in the US encompass large credits for the purchase of military equipment and compensatory transfers to countries, such as Israel and Egypt, arising from commitments made by the US Government in order to facilitate the achievement of certain foreign policy objectives.

(b) In the recent past the British Government has used funds allocated for overseas development to subsidise British firms competing for large contracts in certain countries.

The use of public funds for these purposes is a perfectly legitimate element of foreign or commercial policy, but it is clearly not appropriate to characterise such expenditures as foreign aid. No doubt some development benefits accrue to the recipient countries, but that is hardly the primary purpose of the transfers.

The examples given suggest that we need to define what we mean by 'foreign aid' more specifically. The definition used in OECD statistics on aid flows is as follows: foreign aid consists of all financial and real transfers of resources whose primary purpose is to further socio-economic development in the recipient country and for which the gift or 'grant' element comprises at least 25% of the value of the transfer. The reason for the last part of the definition is that a substantial proportion of foreign aid takes the form of loans on special terms—i.e. with low interest rates and/or long repayment periods.

Source: *The Economic Review* January 1984

Figure 37.4

The effectiveness of aid

Direct attempts to improve living standards through aid have had some success. Aid for basic services (health, nutrition, family planning, education, housing) is an area where donors have acted on the lessons of experience: while aid in the past financed metropolitan hospitals used by urban middle classes, or not-so-low cost housing that the poor could not afford, it is more likely today to be used for rural health clinics and paramedical workers, or "sites-and-services" schemes which do benefit poor people. Similarly in nutrition, family planning, and education, methods of reaching the poor with effective services are now known and being put into practice.

Efforts to improve the productivity, income, and assets of poor people are harder to assess. Only a fraction of aid goes into schemes that are directly poverty-oriented, and one must therefore look at the effects on the poor of a whole range of aid endeavours. To a large extent, the success of aid in reaching the poor is bound up with the success of aid for rural development. The record of aid for rural development, like that of rural development in general, is much better in South Asia than in Africa. In Africa only a small proportion of aid—much of it rather unsuccessful—has gone into small-scale agriculture or livestock investment, and aid for research on food crops has been relatively neglected, compared with cash crops.

Source: *Finance & Development* (IMF) March 1986

Figure 37.1
Figures may be presented in gross or net form. A net figure suggests that something has been deducted from a gross, or unmodifed figure. For example, investment may be expressed as a gross or net figure: the gross figure would include replacement investment which does not increase capital stock, whereas the net investment would not include it.

1. What is the difference between 'gross' and 'net' aid?
2. For which types of aid in the table will the distinction between gross and net be meaningless? Explain your answer.

Figure 37.2
The way that countries are ranked for the basis of comparison may give different results. Countries may be put into rank order for many different purposes, for example to compare living standards, inflation rates, investment levels, etc. The statistics used will alter the rank ordering. For example, the USA has the world's largest GDP, but not the largest GDP per capita.

3. Which country in the table probably gave the greatest amount of aid in 1985, and why?
4. Where would the country in your answer to question 3 stand when aid as a percentage of donor GDP is taken as the criterion for measuring aid contributions?

Figure 37.3
Complex passages may have relatively straightforward meanings. It is easy to be put off by long words and jargon used in economics: in some cases complex language may disguise a relatively straightforward point, whereas in other cases straightforward language may be used to put forward a complex argument.

5. Which part of the passage is saying that much US foreign 'aid' is given for military and political reasons?

Figure 37.4
Economic analysis by organizations may reflect their policy objectives. Organizations like the Treasury, the Confederation of British Industry and the United Nations will have particular policy objectives that they are pursuing. It is important to be aware of the source of data because the data may give a good indication of the policy objectives of the organization that presented it.

6. Can it be inferred from the passage that the IMF wishes more aid to be channelled into large-scale projects such as dams and urban hospitals? Explain your answer.

APPLYING ECONOMIC PRINCIPLES

1. (a) What is the difference between 'bilateral aid' and 'multilateral aid'? Refer to Figure 37.1. (b) What percentage of aid in 1983 was bilateral aid? (c) For what reasons may nations prefer to give aid on a bilateral basis?

2. Refer to Figure 37.2. (a) What percentage of the OECD countries shown gave a higher percentage of their GNP in aid in 1985 than in 1970? (b) Which country made the biggest increase in aid relative to its GNP between 1975 and 1980? (c) Explain why the cut in the percentage of its GNP aid given by the USA could be of particular importance. (d) (i) Did the USA probably give more or less in aid in real terms in 1985 than in 1970? (ii) Did the USA necessarily give a smaller amount of aid relative to Norway in 1985 compared with 1970? Explain your answers.

3. With reference to Figure 37.3: (a) Give a definition of 'foreign aid'. (b) (i) What alternatives to foreign aid are favoured by critics of aid? (ii) How does the writer respond to the critics? (c) Give two examples of capital transfers from the USA and the UK which may be officially classed as economic aid but which are not directly intended to further the economic development of the countries concerned.

4. Refer to Figure 37.4. (a) What is meant by (i) 'improve the productivity . . . of poor people', (ii) 'rural aid', (iii) 'small-scale agriculture or livestock development', and (iv) 'cash crops'? (b) Why has there been a shift in emphasis in aid from large-scale capital-intensive projects to small-scale labour-intensive projects? (c) What advantages and disadvantages could follow a shift in aid from the development of cash crops to the development of food crops?

5. (a) How does foreign aid provide a conflict for developing nations between current and future consumption? (b) Use a production possibility frontier diagram to illustrate the advantages and disadvantages of switching aid from current expenditure to capital investment.

6. Explain how the use of foreign aid to improve education programmes in deprived rural areas can provide: (a) private benefits for the families in the area; (b) external benefits for the nation as a whole.

FOR FURTHER INVESTIGATION
Charities support the official aid programmes of governments. Obtain information about three of these charities. They are often willing to send out information, and they advertise extensively in the press. Try to find out how they raise funds, how much they raise, and how they spend their income. Write a report on the fund-raising activities and expenditure of the charities. Compare their expenditure on aid with that of governments. Use bar charts, graphs, and so on to present statistical information and support your analysis.

ESSAYS
Refer to the data wherever possible, especially in the first essay.
1. (a) What is meant by 'foreign aid'? (b) What different forms can aid take? (c) How can aid be used to improve the economic development of economically poorer nations?
2. What is the term 'less developed' intended to convey about an economy? Evaluate the following methods of assisting less developed economies: charitable gifts of goods and services (e.g. Live Aid); official aid from governments; credits from international financial institutions. [JMB 6/86]

ACKNOWLEDGEMENTS

The authors and publishers wish to thank the following for permission to reproduce their material:
The Economist, Guardian, Observer, Economic Review, Financial Times, Midland Bank Review, Barclays Bank Review, National Westminster Bank Review, Money Management Review, Economics, British Economy Survey, Weidenfeld & Nicolson.

The following examination boards are also thanked for permission to reproduce questions: University of London School Examinations Board, Joint Matriculation Board, University of Oxford Delegacy of Local Examinations, Southern Universities' Joint Board, Associated Examining Board, Welsh Joint Education Committee, University of Cambridge Local Examination Syndicate.

Every effort has been made to contact the holders of copyright material but if any have been inadvertently overlooked the publishers will make the necessary arrangements at the first opportunity.